Vegi-Mex

Vegetarian Mexican
Recipes

by

Shayne and Lee Fischer

**GOLDEN
WEST** ☼
PUBLISHERS

Front cover photo © 1997 Larry Lee/Westlight

More books by Shayne & Lee Fischer

by Shayne and Lee Fischer:
Low-Fat Mexican Recipes
Berry Lovers Cook Book
Burrito Lovers Cook Book

by Shayne Fischer:
Bean Lovers Cook Book
Wholly Frijoles (The Whole Bean Cook Book)

Refried Anasazi Beans recipe courtesy Joyce Waller of the Adobe Milling Co., Dove Creek, Colorado.

Library of Congress Cataloguing in Publication Data
Fischer, Shayne
　　　Vegi-Mex: Vegetarian Mexican Recipes / by Shayne & Lee Fischer.
　　　　　p.　 cm.
　　　Includes index and glossary
　　　ISBN 1-885590-14-8
　　　1. Vegetarian cookery.　 2. Cookery, Mexican I. Fischer, Lee
　　　　II. Title
　　TX837.F478　1997　　　　　　　　　　　97-46754
　　641.5'636—dc21　　　　　　　　　　　　CIP

Printed in the United States of America

5th Printing © 2002

Information in this book is deemed to be authentic and accurate by authors and publisher. However, they disclaim any liability incurred in connection with the use of information appearing in this book.

Golden West Publishers
4113 N. Longview Ave.
Phoenix, AZ 85014, USA
(602) 265-4392

Visit our website: goldenwestpublishers.com

Vegi-Mex
Vegetarian Mexican Recipes

Table of Contents

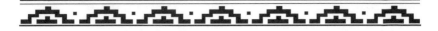

Introduction

You don't have to be a vegetarian to enjoy the wonderful recipes in **Vegi-Mex.** Mexican foods, by their very nature, have rich, bold flavors. Eliminating meats from the recipes which traditionally call for them, allows the cook to experiment with Mexican cooking basics and come up with satisfying, alternative treats.

Yes, you can enjoy Mexican food without eating meat, fish or fowl. A vegetarian diet, which is usually lower in calories, will provide you with more fiber and plenty of protein and calcium, too. Meat alternatives, such as tofu and TVP (texturized vegetable protein) can be sliced, diced and spiced in many tantalizing ways. Mexican foods derive their tastiness from a variety of ingredients, notably hot and spicy peppers, herbs and fantastic sauces.

Vegetarians fall into two basic camps, *lacto-ovo vegetarians* and *vegans.* A lacto-ovo diet allows for consumption of dairy and egg products. A vegan diet is free from all animal derived products. Many magazines and cookbooks are dedicated to vegetarian lifestyles. The purpose of this book is to introduce you to meatless Mexican cooking.

Many of the lacto-ovo recipes in **Vegi-Mex** can be adapted to become vegan recipes. For instance, try substituting rice milk, soy milk or nut milk for cow's milk. Rice milk is milder than soy milk, and nut milks, such as almond milk, are beginning to enjoy new-found popularity. Similarly, soy cheeses can be substituted for any of the cheeses listed as recipe ingredients. As melting and baking properties may vary, you will probably want to experiment with the many different varieties available on the market. Puréed tofu can be substituted for cream cheese, and soy margarine can be used instead of butter.

As public awareness grows regarding the many benefits of vegetarian diets, natural foods stores and supermarkets carry an ever-increasing array of meat and dairy substitutes and alternatives. Even available now are products such as vegetarian "ground beef," a plant derived meat replacement.

The American Dietetic Association has affirmed that a vegetarian diet can meet all known nutrient needs. Excellent sources of protein include low fat dairy products, peas, garbanzos, beans, potatoes, greens and corn. Sources of calcium include low fat milk and dairy, tofu, broccoli, almonds and sunflower seeds.

In the following food pyramid, keep in mind that the five food groups at the base provide adequate amounts of all essential nutrients, except Vitamin B-12, which is available in fortified plant foods and supplements, as well as dairy and eggs.

The bottom line is, people today are overwhelmed by the variety of foods available. Ethnic foods, such as Mexican foods, add to our spice of life. Many Mexican foods traditionally are animal free, and most of the others can be adapted, as you will see. We wish you good health and good eating.

Shayne & Lee Fischer

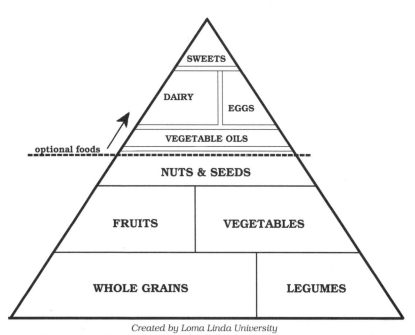

Created by Loma Linda University

Glossary

Arroz: Rice

Burro/Burrito: Flour tortillas filled with a mixture of choice, folded and rolled and frequently topped with a variety of salsas.

Chiles: See *Chile Glossary* page 89.

Chiles Rellenos: Cheese-stuffed peppers, battered and fried.

Cilantro: Also known as Chinese Parsley. Cilantro is the leaf of the Coriander plant. The leaves, which can be used fresh or dried, impart a distinctive, almost "soapy" flavor.

Cumin: A key spice in many Mexican foods, cumin is also used in many Indian dishes, particularly curry mixtures.

Enchiladas: Rolled corn tortillas filled with cheese or vegetables, topped with melted cheese and a green or red chile sauce.

Ensalada: Salad

Flan: A caramel custard dessert.

Frijoles: Beans

Guacamole: An avocado mixture that can be served as an appetizer with dips, or as an accompaniment to main dishes, or as a main ingredients, as in *Guacamole Tostadas.*

Huevo: Egg

Huevos Rancheros: Mexican country-style eggs.

Jicama (hee-cah-mah): A tuber resembling a large, brown potato, similar in texture and taste to a water chestnut.

Lacto-ovo: A vegetarian diet which contains dairy and egg products.

Masa Harina: Corn flour

Nachos: Tortilla chips topped with a variety of ingredients, usually served as an appetizer.

Papas: Potatoes

Picante: Hot, as in spicy foods.

Quesadilla: A crisped corn or flour tortilla folded over with cheese and other ingredients inside.

Queso: Cheese

Salsa Verde: A green sauce made with tomatillos.

Soymage®: A replacement for dairy cheese.

Taco: A tortilla, usually corn, that is folded in half, baked or fried, and filled with a variety of ingredients. Soft tacos are made with heated corn or flour tortillas.

Tofu: Protein rich soybean curd, free from saturated fat and cholesterol. Can be crumbled, sliced, diced or puréed.

Tomatillo: A small, firm green tomato-like fruit which is covered with a papery husk. Used in *Salsa Verde.*

Tortillas: A thin pancake-like "bread" which can be made of flour or corn. Tortillas are utilized in countless Mexican dishes.

Tostada: A corn tortilla, served flat and crisped (baked or fried), layered with refried beans, lettuce, tomatoes, etc.

TVP: Texturized vegetable protein. Can be substituted for ground meats.

Vegan: A diet free from all animal derived products.

Appetizers

What could be more of a traditional Mexican food appetizer than salsa and chips? Whether you're entertaining or dining alone you'll love the taste of these chips and enjoy the guilt-free satisfaction of knowing you're snacking the low-fat way. Unlike restaurant or many commercial chips these chips are baked, not fried, thereby eliminating fat-laden oils.

Baked Corn Tortilla Chips

12 CORN TORTILLAS, frozen

Preheat oven to 400°. Stack tortillas three-at-a-time and cut into wedge shapes. Arrange in single layer on cookie sheet. Bake on top rack of oven for approximately three minutes or until crisp. To avoid overbaking, check frequently and remove from oven at first signs of browning.

Savory suggestion: For spicy Mexican-flavored chips, slightly moisten tortillas and sprinkle, before baking, with garlic salt, chili powder and ground cayenne pepper.

Flour Tortilla Chips

Lard-free flour tortillas are available in most markets.

10 (7- inch) FLOUR TORTILLAS

Preheat oven to 400°. Stack tortillas five-at-a-time and cut into wedge shapes. Arrange in single layer on cookie sheet. Bake on top rack of oven for approximately two minutes or until crisp. To avoid overbaking, check frequently and remove from oven after initial browning. Serve warm.

Savory suggestion: Using spray bottle, slightly moisten unbaked tortillas with water and sprinkle with salt, garlic powder and chili powder.

Salsas are a key ingredient in many Mexican foods. Spanish for sauce, salsas can be used as a dip for appetizers or as an accompaniment for main and side dishes.

Table Salsa

4 med. TOMATOES, finely chopped
1 can (8 oz.) TOMATO SAUCE
1 can (4 oz.) diced GREEN CHILES, drained
3 GREEN ONIONS, chopped
1 clove GARLIC, crushed
1/4 tsp. OREGANO
1/4 tsp. ground CUMIN
1/4 tsp. CHILI POWDER
SALT and PEPPER to taste

Combine all ingredients in glass bowl. Cover and refrigerate. For best results make the day before.

Makes 3 cups.

Fiery Salsa

2 lg. TOMATOES, diced
1 can (8 oz.) TOMATO SAUCE
1 tsp. CHILI POWDER
1/2 tsp. GARLIC SALT
1/2 tsp. OREGANO
1/4 tsp. ground CUMIN
2 JALAPEÑO PEPPERS, seeded and diced
1 can (4 oz.) diced GREEN CHILES, drained

Combine all ingredients in glass bowl. Cover and refrigerate overnight.

Makes approximately 2 cups.

Cilantro Salsa

Cilantro is also known as Chinese parsley and coriander. Both the leaves and tender stems can be used in fresh or cooked dishes.

1 can (15 oz.) ITALIAN PLUM TOMATOES, drained, chopped
1 can (8 oz.) TOMATO SAUCE
1/4 cup fresh CILANTRO, finely chopped
1 can (4 oz.) diced GREEN CHILES, drained
1/2 tsp. ground CUMIN
1/2 tsp. GARLIC SALT
1/4 tsp. ONION SALT
PEPPER to taste

Combine all ingredients and chill for several hours before serving.

Makes 4 cups.

Easy Salsa

For the busy cook, this salsa can be made in a jiffy!

1 can (15 oz.) STEWED TOMATOES, crushed
1 can (8 oz.) TOMATO SAUCE
1 can (7 oz.) diced GREEN CHILES
1 can (2 oz.) chopped BLACK OLIVES
1 sm. ONION, diced
1/2 tsp. GARLIC SALT
1/2 tsp. SUGAR
1/4 tsp. CAYENNE PEPPER

Combine all ingredients and chill for several hours before serving.

Makes 4 cups.

Salsa Picante
(Hot Salsa)

The best neutralizers to the heat in hot salsas are dairy products, such as milk, sour cream, yogurt or ice cream.

3 med. TOMATOES, chopped
1 GREEN BELL PEPPER, seeded and chopped
1 med. ONION, chopped
1 crushed CHILTEPIN
2 sm. YELLOW CHILES, seeded and diced
1/2 tsp. GARLIC SALT
1 Tbsp. LIME or LEMON JUICE
4 Tbsp. chopped fresh CILANTRO

Combine all ingredients and refrigerate until thoroughly chilled.

Makes 2 cups.

Salsa Verde
(Green Salsa)

6 ANAHEIM CHILES, roasted, seeded and diced
1/2 cup fresh CILANTRO, chopped
1 sm. ONION, chopped
1 clove GARLIC, pressed
1/2 tsp. ground CUMIN
1 Tbsp. LEMON JUICE
SALT and PEPPER to taste

Place all ingredients in blender and blend until desired thickness. Refrigerate for several hours.

Makes 2 cups.

Salsa Blanca

1 pint COTTAGE CHEESE
3 Tbsp. MAYONNAISE
1 cup CHUNKY SALSA

Combine all ingredients. Serve with tortilla chips or use as a dip for fresh vegetables.

Black Bean Dip

Black beans are also called turtle beans. These smoky-tasting beans lend themselves to salsas, dips, salads and much more.

1 can (15 oz.) BLACK BEANS, drained
2 cloves GARLIC
2 Tbsp. LEMON JUICE
1/2 tsp. SALT
4 Tbsp. SALSA

In a food processor or blender, purée all ingredients together. Serve with tortilla chips, crackers or wedges of baked pita bread.

Creamy Bean Dip

This easy-to-prepare bean dip can be served heated or chilled.

1 can (15 oz.) whole PINTO BEANS, drained
1 pkg. (8 oz.) CREAM CHEESE, room temperature
4 Tbsp. SALSA
1/2 tsp. GARLIC SALT

Combine all ingredients in a food processor and blend to desired consistency. Serve with tortilla chips or spread on tostada shells and place under the broiler for just a minute to crisp.

Nutty Bean Dip

This dip is delicious when served with vegetables, chips, or lahvosh.

1 can (15 oz.) VEGETARIAN REFRIED BEANS
1 stalk CELERY, diced
1/2 cup chopped WALNUTS
3 GREEN ONIONS, chopped
3 Tbsp. MAYONNAISE
1/2 tsp. GARLIC SALT
1/2 tsp. CHILI POWDER

Combine all ingredients together and mix well. Refrigerate before serving.

Confetti Bean Dip

This dip is so tasty you may want to serve it as a side dish.

1 can (15 oz.) BLACK BEANS, drained and rinsed
1 can (15 oz.) KIDNEY BEANS, drained and rinsed
2 lg. TOMATOES, diced
1/4 cup diced ONIONS
1 CUCUMBER, peeled and diced
1 can (4 oz.) diced GREEN CHILES
1/2 cup chopped fresh CILANTRO
1/2 tsp. GARLIC SALT
1/4 tsp. PEPPER
1 Tbsp. LEMON JUICE

Combine all ingredients in a glass bowl and refrigerate for at least one hour. Serve chilled.

Spicy Jicama Sticks

Jicama (HEE-kah-mah) is often referred to as the Mexican potato. *Its water chestnut-type texture and taste is delicious both raw and cooked. A good source of vitamin C and potassium, it can be found in most supermarkets and in Mexican markets. Try these tasty snacks in place of tortilla chips.*

**1 med. JICAMA
GARLIC SALT
CHILI POWDER
CAYENNE PEPPER**

Wash and peel jicama. Cut into sticks or chips and rinse in cold water. Drain and sprinkle lightly with seasonings, using cayenne sparingly. These make great and unusual appetizers for your relish tray.

Papas en Escabeche
(Pickled Potatoes)

**1 can (15 oz.) WHOLE WHITE SMALL POTATOES
2 Tbsp. VINEGAR
2 GREEN ONIONS, chopped
1 can (4 oz.) diced JALAPEÑOS
1/4 tsp. GARLIC POWDER
SALT and PEPPER to taste**

Drain potatoes and place in glass bowl. Add vinegar, onion and jalapeños. Season with garlic, salt and pepper. Cover and refrigerate. Allow potatoes to marinate overnight. Serve chilled.

Stuffed Jalapeños

2 cans (4 oz. each) WHOLE JALAPEÑOS
4 oz. CREAM CHEESE
1 GREEN ONION, finely chopped
SALT to taste

Drain jalapeños, slice lengthwise and place on a platter. Combine cream cheese, onion and salt and mix thoroughly. Spread cream cheese mixture into chiles, cover and refrigerate until ready to serve.

Spicy Vegetable Medley

1 med. JICAMA peeled and diced in 1/2-inch chunks
1 can (15 oz.) WHOLE WHITE SMALL POTATOES
8 oz. BABY CARROTS, fresh or frozen
2 cups CAULIFLOWER FLORETS, parboiled
1 med. ONION, sliced
1 GREEN BELL PEPPER, sliced
1 can (4 oz.) diced JALAPEÑOS
1/4 cup VINEGAR
2 Tbsp. LEMON JUICE
1/2 tsp. SUGAR
1/2 tsp. GARLIC SALT
1/4 tsp. PEPPER

In a large mixing bowl combine all ingredients. Mix thoroughly so vegetables are evenly coated with marinade. Refrigerate overnight. Before serving, toss vegetables lightly to redistribute marinade.

Tortilla Roll-ups

1 pkg. (8 oz.) CREAM CHEESE, softened
2 Tbsp. SOUR CREAM
3 GREEN ONION, finely minced
1 can (4 oz.) diced GREEN CHILES
1/4 tsp. GARLIC SALT
6 (10-inch) FLOUR TORTILLAS

Blend together all ingredients except flour tortillas. Spread mixture evenly over each tortilla and roll tightly. Cover with plastic wrap to keep from drying out and chill thoroughly. Slice each roll-up into half-inch slices.

Veggie Rolls

1 pkg. (8 oz.) CREAM CHEESE, softened
1/2 cup MAYONNAISE
2 TOMATOES, finely chopped
1/2 cup shredded CARROTS
1/4 cup finely diced GREEN ONIONS
1/4 cup finely diced CUCUMBERS
1/4 cup finely diced CELERY
1 can (4 oz.) diced GREEN CHILES,
    drained
1/2 tsp. GARLIC SALT
1/4 tsp. CAYENNE PEPPER
6 (10-inch) FLOUR TORTILLAS

Blend cream cheese and mayonnaise together. Add vegetables and seasonings. Spread mixture evenly over tortillas. Roll up and wrap in plastic wrap. Refrigerate for at least 2 hours. Slice into 1-inch sections and serve.

Veggie Quesadillas

These delightful appetizers can be baked in the oven or heated to a crisp on the stove, in a frying pan or hot griddle.

4 (10-inch) FLOUR TORTILLAS
1 cup shredded COLBY JACK CHEESE
1 GREEN BELL PEPPER, sliced
1 can (4 oz.) diced GREEN CHILES, drained
1 sm. ONION, finely chopped
1 TOMATO, diced
1 can (2 oz.) sliced BLACK OLIVES

If baking in the oven, preheat to 350°. Place tortillas on cookie sheet. Top with cheese, bell pepper, chiles, onion, tomato and olives. Bake for two minutes, fold in half, and continue baking until crisp, approximately three more minutes. Remove to serving platter. For faster and crispier results, use the broiler method: place loaded tortillas (still on cookie sheet) under broiler. As soon as cheese starts to melt, fold tortillas and broil until crisp (watch carefully as cooking time will be greatly reduced). Cut into wedges and serve with **SALSA, SOUR CREAM** and **GUACAMOLE.**

Corn Crisps

6 CORN TORTILLAS
3/4 cup shredded LONGHORN CHEESE
3 Tbsp. diced GREEN CHILES
1 TOMATO, diced

Preheat oven to 400°. Place tortillas on cookie sheet and sprinkle with shredded cheese and chiles. Bake for two minutes, or until cheese bubbles. Remove to serving platter(s) and sprinkle with diced tomato. Serve with **SALSA** and **SOUR CREAM.**

Avocado Dip

3/4 cup COTTAGE CHEESE
1/2 cup SOUR CREAM
1 ripe AVOCADO, mashed
1 1/2 tsp. LEMON JUICE
1/2 tsp. GARLIC SALT
1/4 tsp. PEPPER
3 Tbsp. SALSA
4 Tbsp. diced GREEN CHILES

In a food processor, blend cottage cheese, sour cream, avocado, lemon juice, garlic salt and pepper until smooth. Add salsa and green chiles and pulse briefly. Transfer to serving bowl. May be served immediately or chilled until ready for use (this will keep in the refrigerator for one or two days). Serve with tortilla chips and your favorite fresh vegetables.

Guacamole

2 ripe AVOCADOS
1/3 cup finely chopped ONION
1 lg. TOMATO, diced
1 Tbsp. MAYONNAISE
1 Tbsp. fresh LEMON JUICE
1/2 tsp. GARLIC SALT
2 Tbsp. SALSA

Cut avocados in half and remove pits. Scoop flesh into a glass bowl and mash with a fork. Add remaining ingredients and mix thoroughly. Allow to chill before serving.

Suggestion: To keep guacamole from turning brown, save pits from avocados and push them into the dip. Remove before serving.

Nachos Grande

TORTILLA CHIPS
1 can (15 oz.) VEGETARIAN REFRIED BEANS
3/4 cup shredded LONGHORN CHEESE
3/4 cup shredded JACK CHEESE
1 can (4 oz.) diced GREEN CHILES
1 med. TOMATO, diced
3 GREEN ONIONS, chopped
1/4 cup sliced BLACK OLIVES

Preheat oven to 350°. On a large oven-proof platter, layer tortilla chips, beans, cheese and green chiles. Bake for five minutes or until cheese melts. Remove from oven and sprinkle with tomatoes and onions. Top with black olives. Serve with **SALSA** on the side. Other excellent toppings include **SOUR CREAM, AVO-CADO** and **sliced JALAPEÑOS.**

Pico de Gallo

Spanish for "rooster's beak," pico de gallo (PEE-koh day GI-yoh) is a relish made of finely chopped ingredients. This condiment was so named because it was once purportedly eaten with the thumb and finger, an action that resembles a rooster's pecking beak.

3 lg. TOMATOES
4 JALAPEÑOS
1 lg. ONION
1 lg. GREEN BELL PEPPER
2 cloves GARLIC
1 bunch fresh CILANTRO

1/2 Tbsp. SALT
1 tsp. BLACK PEPPER
1/4 cup COLD WATER
2 Tbsp. VINEGAR
1 LIME

On a cutting board, finely chop tomatoes, jalapeños, onion, bell pepper, garlic and cilantro. Place all in glass bowl and mix together. Add salt, pepper, water and vinegar. Squeeze the juice from the lime into the mixture and mix thoroughly. Chill before serving.

Baked Fiesta Dip

2 cans (15 oz. each) VEGETARIAN REFRIED BEANS
1 can (4 oz.) diced GREEN CHILES
2 JALAPEÑOS, finely chopped
1 1/2 cups shredded JACK CHEESE
1 ONION, chopped
1 GREEN BELL PEPPER, chopped
1 can (4 oz.) sliced BLACK OLIVES
1 TOMATO, chopped
3 GREEN ONIONS, chopped
TORTILLA CHIPS

Combine beans, chiles and jalapeños and spread on large oven-proof platter (or pizza pan). Sprinkle with cheese. Add onion, bell pepper and olives. Bake at 325° for 15 minutes. Top with tomatoes and green onions and serve with tortilla chips.

Eight-Layer Dip

1 can (15 oz.) VEGETARIAN REFRIED BEANS
1 cup COTTAGE CHEESE
1 cup SOUR CREAM
1/2 cup CHUNKY SALSA
1 can (4 oz.) diced GREEN CHILES, drained
1 AVOCADO, chopped
1 TOMATO, chopped
1/2 cup shredded CHEDDAR CHEESE
1 can (2 oz.) sliced BLACK OLIVES
TORTILLA CHIPS

Spread beans evenly in a 9-inch pie plate. Spread cottage cheese over beans. Combine sour cream and salsa and layer over cottage cheese. Cover and chill for at least two hours. Just before serving sprinkle with chiles, avocado and tomato and top with cheddar cheese and olives. Serve with tortilla chips.

Breakfasts

Pan Potatoes

2 Tbsp. MARGARINE
1 med. ONION, chopped
1 GREEN BELL PEPPER, chopped
4 POTATOES, peeled and diced

1/2 tsp. GARLIC SALT
1/4 tsp. PEPPER
1/4 tsp. ground OREGANO
1/4 tsp. CHILI POWDER

In a large frying pan or skillet, sauté onions and bell pepper in margarine. When onions and pepper are tender, add diced potatoes and seasonings. Cover and cook over medium heat, stirring occasionally. When potatoes have softened, uncover and fry to desired crispness. Serve with plenty of **SALSA.**

Serves 6-8.

Huevos con Chiles Verde

(Eggs with Green Chiles)

This scrambled egg dish is also a great filling for breakfast burritos. For a spicier morning dish, substitute jalapeños for the green chiles.

1 Tbsp. MARGARINE
1 can (4 oz.) diced GREEN CHILES, drained
1 can (4 oz.) sliced MUSHROOMS, drained
3 Tbsp. chopped ONIONS
6 EGGS
1/2 tsp. GARLIC SALT
PEPPER to taste
1 sm. TOMATO, finely chopped

In a skillet, sauté chiles, mushrooms and onions in margarine. Beat eggs and add garlic salt and pepper. Stir eggs into chile and onions and cook until eggs reach desired consistency. Sprinkle tomatoes over top and serve warm.

Serves 4.

Huevos Rancheros

4 (7-inch) FLOUR TORTILLAS
1 1/2 cups cooked, mashed PINTO BEANS
4 EGGS
1 cup shredded CHEDDAR CHEESE
CHUNKY SALSA

Arrange tortillas on cookie sheet. Spread beans on tortillas. Fry eggs as desired (over-easy, scrambled, sunny-side up) in non-stick skillet. Leave eggs slightly undercooked as they will be getting additional heat when broiled. Arrange eggs over beans. Sprinkle cheese evenly over eggs. Place under broiler just long enough to melt cheese. Remove to serving platters and add salsa to taste.

Serves 4.

Note: *Green Chile Sauce* (see page 54) or *Red Chile Sauce* (see page 55) can be ladled over eggs before placing under the broiler.

Torta de Huevo
(Omelet)

4 EGGS
1 Tbsp. MILK
1 Tbsp. MARGARINE
1/2 cup chopped TOMATO
1/2 cup sliced MUSHROOMS
1/4 cup chopped ONION
2 JALAPEÑOS, chopped
1/2 cup shredded JACK CHEESE

Beat eggs and milk together until creamy. Heat margarine in a large skillet. Pour in eggs and cook without stirring over a low heat until underside is browned. Place the remaining ingredients on one half of omelet; fold unfilled half over. Continue to cook over a low heat until cheese melts.

Serves 2.

Chile Relleno Bake

This meal can be served at any time of the day and is great to bring to your next potluck.

1/2 cup NON-FAT DRY MILK
2 cups MILK
3 Tbsp. FLOUR
6 EGGS, slightly beaten
1/4 cup SALSA
NONSTICK VEGETABLE SPRAY
6 CORN TORTILLAS
1 can (7 oz.) diced GREEN CHILES
1 cup shredded CHEDDAR CHEESE
1 cup shredded JACK CHEESE
1/2 cup finely chopped ONION

Preheat oven to 325°. Combine dry milk and milk and stir in flour. Blend thoroughly. Add eggs and salsa. Lightly spray a 9 x 13 baking dish with vegetable spray. Layer with corn tortillas, green chiles, cheeses and onion. Pour egg mixture on top. Bake for 1 hour. Remove from oven and let set for 10 minutes before serving.

Serves 10.

Torta de Chile Verde

(Green Chile Omelet)

6 EGGS
6 Tbsp. WATER
1/2 tsp. SALT
1/4 tsp. PAPRIKA
1/4 tsp. PEPPER
1 tsp. MARGARINE
2 ANAHEIM or NEW MEXICO CHILES, seeded and sliced
3/4 cup shredded CHEDDAR CHEESE

Separate eggs, placing egg whites in a small bowl and yolks in a large bowl. Beat egg yolks thoroughly. Add water and seasonings to the egg yolks and mix well. Whip egg whites until stiff. Fold egg whites into yolks. In a nonstick skillet, heat margarine and add egg mixture. Cook over medium heat until edges begin to brown (surface of eggs should just begin to set). Add chiles and cheese and fold over omelet. Continue to cook until cheese melts. Do not overcook. Remove to serving platter and cut into wedges. Serve with **SALSA** and warm **TORTILLAS**

Serves 6.

Corn Pudding

4 cups MILK
3/4 cup CORNMEAL
1/2 cup MAPLE SYRUP

2 EGGS
1/2 tsp. CINNAMON
1/3 cup BROWN SUGAR

In a saucepan, heat milk over medium heat until very hot, but not boiling. Stir cornmeal into milk and simmer gently for 20 minutes, stirring occasionally. In a medium bowl, combine remaining ingredients. Add to cornmeal mixture and blend thoroughly. Pour into a lightly oiled oven-proof baking dish. Bake in a 325° oven for 1 hour. Let stand to set before serving. Serve warm or chilled.

Serves 6.

Breakfast Burritos

A great way to warm up on a cool morning! Holding these burritos while you eat them warms your hands and your soul.

2 tsp. MARGARINE
1/2 sm. ONION, chopped
1/2 RED BELL PEPPER, chopped
1 can (4 oz.) diced GREEN
    CHILES, drained
4 lg. EGGS
SALT and PEPPER to taste
SALSA, to taste
4 (10-inch) FLOUR TORTILLAS

In a skillet, heat margarine and sauté onions and red pepper until tender. Add chiles and continue to cook. Beat eggs, add salt and pepper and pour over skillet mixture. Scramble over medium heat. As eggs solidify add salsa. Warm tortillas. Place equal amounts of egg mixture onto each tortilla and roll burrito style.

Serves 4.

Morning Wraps

1/2 sm. ONION, chopped
2 tsp. MARGARINE
1 can (4 oz.) diced GREEN
    CHILES, drained
4 lg. EGGS
1/2 tsp. GARLIC SALT

3/4 cup shredded LONGHORN
    CHEESE
4 (10-inch) FLOUR TORTILLAS
ALFALFA SPROUTS
1 med. TOMATO, chopped
SALSA

In a skillet, sauté onions in margarine until tender. Add chiles. Beat eggs, add garlic salt and pour over onions and chiles. Scramble over medium heat, sprinkle with cheese and cook until eggs are desired consistency. Warm tortillas. Place equal amounts of egg mixture onto each tortilla. Add sprouts, tomato and salsa. Roll up burrito style.

Serves 4.

Soups & Salads

Gazpacho

4 TOMATOES, chopped
1 lg. CUCUMBER, peeled and chopped
1 GREEN BELL PEPPER, seeded and chopped
1 bunch GREEN ONIONS, finely chopped
3 cups TOMATO JUICE
1 clove GARLIC, minced
1/2 tsp. OREGANO
1/2 tsp. TABASCO®
2 Tbsp. LEMON JUICE
SALT and PEPPER to taste
Fresh CILANTRO

Mix all ingredients, except cilantro, in a large glass bowl. Cover and chill for at least four hours. Pour into individual bowls and garnish with fresh cilantro.

Serves 4.

Tortilla Soup

6 CORN TORTILLAS
2 cups VEGETABLE BROTH
2 cups WATER
1 ONION, chopped
1 clove GARLIC, minced
3 CARROTS, cut into
    1-inch strips
2 stalks CELERY, sliced
1 can (4 oz.) diced GREEN
    CHILES
1/8 tsp. ground CUMIN
1/2 tsp. OREGANO
1/4 cup chopped CILANTRO
SALT and PEPPER to taste
1/2 cup shredded JACK
    CHEESE

Cut tortillas into thin strips and bake on a cookie sheet in a 400° oven until crisp. In a saucepan, combine vegetable broth, water, vegetables and seasonings and simmer for 30 minutes. When ready to serve, place equal amounts of tortilla strips in bottom of each bowl and ladle soup over top. Garnish with cheese.

Serves 6.

Pinto Bean Soup

1 lb. dried **PINTO BEANS**
WATER
1 lg. **ONION**, chopped
1 clove **GARLIC**, minced
1 **JALAPEÑO**, seeded and chopped
1/2 tsp. **OREGANO**
1/4 tsp. ground **CUMIN**
dash of **CAYENNE**
1/2 tsp. **BLACK PEPPER**
SALT to taste

Sort through beans and wash thoroughly. Cover with water and allow to soak overnight. Drain and rinse. Cover beans with fresh water. Add remaining ingredients (except salt) and bring to a boil. Reduce heat to low and cover with tight-fitting lid. Continue to cook until beans are tender (approximately 2-3 hours). Stir at least every 30 minutes and add water as necessary (beans should always be covered with liquid). Add salt just before serving.

Serves 6.

Serving suggestion: Garnish with **chopped TOMATOES, sprigs of CILANTRO** and a sprinkle of **shredded CHEESE.**

Chili Bean Soup

1/3 cup FLOUR
2 Tbsp. VEGETABLE OIL
3 cups WATER
3 Tbsp. CHILI POWDER
1 tsp. GARLIC SALT
1 can (15 oz.) PINTO BEANS, drained
1 can (16 oz.) TOMATOES
1 can (4 oz.) diced GREEN CHILES
1 ONION, chopped
2 CARROTS, sliced
2 stalks CELERY, sliced

In a large saucepan, brown flour in oil. Add water, chili powder and garlic salt and mix well. Cover and cook briefly over low heat. Stir in remaining ingredients. Cover and simmer for 30 minutes.

Serves 6.

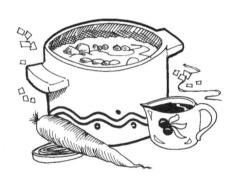

Verde y Blanco Sopa
(Green and White Soup)

This healthy soup combines broccoli and cauliflower, both of which are high in vitamin C and iron.

1 lb. BROCCOLI FLORETS
1 lb. CAULIFLOWER FLORETS
8 cups WATER
2 ANAHEIM or NEW MEXICO CHILES
1 ONION, quartered
4 stalks CELERY, cut into 1/2-inch pieces
4 CARROTS, cut into 1/2-inch pieces
1 BAY LEAF
1/2 tsp. GARLIC SALT
1/2 tsp. CAYENNE PEPPER
1/2 cup chopped fresh CILANTRO
1/2 tsp. ground CUMIN
2 ZUCCHINIS, cut into 1/2-inch pieces
SALT and PEPPER to taste

In a large pot, cover broccoli and cauliflower florets with water and bring to a boil. Cook for 10 minutes. Add seeded and sliced chiles (be sure to wear rubber gloves and do not touch your face!) Add onion, celery, carrots, bay leaf and seasonings. Reduce heat, cover pot and simmer for 30 minutes. Add zucchini and salt and pepper and continue simmering until vegetables are tender. Remove bay leaf before serving.

Serves 8.

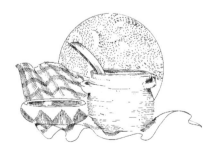

Sopa de Papas

(Potato Soup)

6 lg. POTATOES
1 ONION, chopped
1 GREEN BELL PEPPER, chopped
1 can (4 oz.) diced GREEN CHILES
2 stalks CELERY, sliced
2 cloves GARLIC, minced
6 cups WATER
1 can (14.5 oz.) VEGETABLE BROTH
SALT and PEPPER to taste
1/4 tsp. CAYENNE PEPPER
2 Tbsp. CORNSTARCH
1/4 cup WATER
1/2 lb. shredded CHEDDAR CHEESE
1 bunch fresh CILANTRO

Wash and cube potatoes (peel if desired). Place potatoes, onion, bell pepper, green chiles, celery, garlic, 6 cups water, broth, salt, pepper and cayenne into a large pot. Bring to a boil, lower heat, cover and simmer until potatoes are tender. Stir occasionally. To thicken, add cornstarch to 1/4 cup water and blend till smooth. Stir into simmering soup. When serving, sprinkle with shredded cheese and fresh cilantro.

Serves 8.

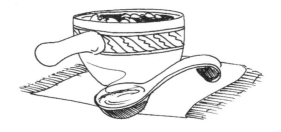

Black Bean & Rice Soup

*Black beans have a black skin, cream-colored flesh
and a sweet, smoky flavor.*

1 ONION, chopped
2 stalks CELERY, diced
2 Tbsp. MARGARINE
1 RED BELL PEPPER, diced
3 CARROTS, diced
4 cups WATER
2 cans (15 oz. each) BLACK BEANS, drained and rinsed
1 cup INSTANT RICE
1 cup SALSA
1/2 tsp. GARLIC SALT
1/2 tsp. OREGANO
1/8 tsp. CAYENNE PEPPER
1/4 tsp. BLACK PEPPER

In a large saucepan, sauté onion and celery in margarine. Add bell pepper, carrots and water and cook until vegetables are tender. Stir in beans, rice, salsa and seasonings. Bring to a boil, turn off heat, cover and let stand 5 minutes.

Serves 6.

Chile Vegetable Soup

This spicy vegan recipe is delicious and easy to make.

1 can (15 oz.) CORN, drained
1 cup SOY MILK
2 Tbsp. SOY MARGARINE
1 cup WATER
1 cup sliced CARROTS
1 cup chopped ONIONS
1 cup sliced ZUCCHINI
1 cup cooked LIMA BEANS
1 cup PEAS
1 can (7 oz.) diced GREEN CHILES
1 tsp. CHILI POWDER
1 tsp. OREGANO
1/2 tsp. GARLIC SALT
1/4 tsp. ground CUMIN

In a blender, blend corn, soy milk and soy margarine. In a large saucepan, combine water, carrots and onions and cook for 5 minutes over medium heat. Add remaining ingredients and stir in corn mixture. Cover and simmer for 15 minutes. Serve garnished with **CILANTRO.**

Serves 8.

Taco Soup

1 cake (8 oz.) firm TOFU, coarsely chopped
1 ONION, chopped
2 Tbsp. VEGETABLE OIL
2 cups WATER
1 can (16 oz.) STEWED TOMATOES, chopped
1 can (16 oz.) KIDNEY BEANS
1 can (8 oz.) TOMATO SAUCE
1 pkg. TACO SEASONING MIX
shredded LONGHORN CHEESE
SOUR CREAM
TORTILLA STRIPS

Sauté tofu and onion in oil in a large saucepan until onion is tender and tofu is browned. Add water, tomatoes, beans, tomato sauce, and taco seasoning. Bring to a boil, reduce heat, cover and simmer for 30 minutes. Ladle into serving bowls and garnish with a sprinkle of cheese, a dollop of sour cream and serve with tortilla strips.

Serves 8.

Sopa de Fideo

(Pasta Soup)

1 pkg. (8 oz.) FIDEO PASTA
1 sm. ONION, finely chopped
2 CARROTS, finely diced
2 stalks CELERY, finely diced
1 can (16 oz.) STEWED
   TOMATOES, chopped

1/2 cup frozen PEAS
4 cups VEGETABLE STOCK
1/2 tsp. SALT
1/4 tsp. GARLIC POWDER
dash TABASCO®

Combine all ingredients in a soup pot. Bring to a boil, stirring occasionally. Continue to cook until pasta is at desired tenderness.

Serves 4.

Ensalada de Pepiño
(Cucumber Salad)

4 CUCUMBERS, peeled and sliced
1 sm. RED ONION, sliced into thin rings
1 cup sliced JICAMA
1 TOMATO, sliced
1 can (4 oz.) BLACK OLIVES
2 Tbsp. SUGAR
2 Tbsp. LEMON JUICE
2 Tbsp. VINEGAR
PAPRIKA

Combine all ingredients, except paprika, and chill. Refrigerate overnight for best flavor. Before serving, toss gently and sprinkle with paprika.

Serves 6.

Jicama Avocado Salad

1 1/2 cups JICAMA strips
1 sm. RED ONION, chopped
1 GREEN BELL PEPPER, seeded and chopped
1 Tbsp. VINEGAR
JUICE of one LEMON
1/4 tsp. CAYENNE PEPPER
SALT and PEPPER to taste

Combine all ingredients. Refrigerate for at least two hours, preferably overnight. Toss gently and garnish with **sliced AVO-CADO** before serving.

Serves 4.

Tofu Taco Salad

1 cake (8 oz.) firm TOFU, cubed
1/2 tsp. GARLIC SALT
1 Tbsp. CHILI POWDER
1 1/2 Tbsp. VEGETABLE OIL
LETTUCE, torn into bite-size pieces
1 CUCUMBER, peeled and diced
1 cup shredded CHEDDAR CHEESE or SOYMAGE®
1 cup CHUNKY SALSA
1 TOMATO, chopped
3 GREEN ONIONS, chopped
1/4 cup sliced BLACK OLIVES
TORTILLA CHIPS, crushed

Sprinkle tofu with garlic salt and chili powder. Sauté in oil until tofu is browned. In a bowl, toss lettuce with tofu, cucumber and cheese. To serve, top with salsa, tomato, green onions, olives and crushed tortilla chips.

Serves 6.

Ensalada de Tres Frijoles
(Three Bean Salad)

1 can (15 oz.) KIDNEY BEANS, drained and rinsed
1 can (15 oz.) BLACK BEANS, drained and rinsed
1 can (15 oz.) GARBANZO BEANS, drained and rinsed
1 RED ONION, thinly sliced
2 stalks CELERY, sliced
1 TOMATO, chopped
1 cup THICK & CHUNKY SALSA
shredded LETTUCE

In a large bowl combine all ingredients (except lettuce). Cover and chill for at least 1 hour. Serve over a bed of shredded lettuce.

Serves 8.

Fiesta Salad

2 TOMATOES, sliced
1 sm. RED ONION, coarsely chopped
1 CUCUMBER, peeled and sliced
1 each GREEN, RED & YELLOW BELL PEPPER, chopped
1 can (4 oz.) diced GREEN CHILES
1/4 cup chopped, fresh CILANTRO
3 Tbsp. SALSA
2 Tbsp. LEMON JUICE
1/2 tsp. GARLIC SALT
1/4 tsp. PEPPER
1/4 tsp. ground CUMIN

Combine all ingredients and chill for at least one hour. Serve with **TORTILLA CHIPS** or on a bed of **LETTUCE.**

Serves 6.

Potato Salad

8 NEW POTATOES, cooked
   and cubed
3 stalks CELERY, diced
2 CARROTS, shredded
3 GREEN ONIONS, sliced
1/2 RED BELL PEPPER, chopped
2 JALAPEÑOS, thinly sliced
1/2 cup MAYONNAISE

1/2 cup SOUR CREAM
1/4 tsp. GARLIC POWDER
1/4 tsp. ground CUMIN
SALT and PEPPER to taste
1 Tbsp. LEMON JUICE
PAPRIKA
fresh CILANTRO

In a large bowl combine potatoes, celery, carrots, onions, bell pepper and jalapeños. In a small bowl blend mayonnaise, sour cream, garlic powder, cumin, salt, pepper and lemon juice. Pour over vegetables and mix thoroughly. Sprinkle with paprika and garnish with cilantro. Chill until ready to serve.

Serves 6.

Corn Salad

2 cans (15 oz. each) CORN, drained
1 can (4 oz.) diced GREEN CHILES, drained
1 sm. RED ONION, sliced into thin rings
4 GREEN ONIONS, chopped
1/2 cup chopped GREEN BELL PEPPER
2 TOMATOES, chopped
1/2 tsp. GARLIC SALT
1/4 tsp. ground CUMIN
1/4 cup VINEGAR
Juice of half of a LEMON
1 Tbsp. SUGAR
LETTUCE LEAVES

Combine all ingredients (except lettuce) in a bowl. Mix thoroughly. Cover and chill well until ready to serve. Toss lightly to redistribute the dressing. Serve on a bed of lettuce leaves.

Serves 6.

Black Bean Salad

1 can (15 oz.) BLACK BEANS, drained and rinsed
1 can (4 oz.) diced GREEN CHILES, drained
4 GREEN ONIONS, cut into 1/2-inch pieces
2 TOMATOES, chopped
1/4 tsp. GARLIC SALT
PEPPER, to taste
1 Tbsp. LEMON JUICE
2 Tbsp. SALSA
1/2 head LETTUCE, shredded

Combine all ingredients in a large bowl and toss well. Refrigerate until thoroughly chilled.

Serves 4.

Tofu & Rice Salad

1 cake (8 oz.) firm TOFU, sliced
2 Tbsp. VEGETABLE OIL
1 sm. ONION, finely chopped
1/2 tsp. CHILI POWDER
1/2 tsp. GARLIC SALT
1/2 tsp. ground CUMIN
1/2 tsp. OREGANO
4 cups cooked RICE
1 head ICEBERG LETTUCE, shredded
1 cup shredded LONGHORN CHEESE
2 TOMATOES, chopped
3 GREEN ONIONS, chopped
SALSA
SOUR CREAM
TORTILLA CHIPS

In a large skillet, over medium heat, brown tofu in oil with onion, chili powder, garlic salt, cumin and oregano. Add cooked rice and stir. Remove from heat and allow to cool. In a large bowl, combine lettuce, cheese, tomatoes and green onions. Add tofu-rice mixture and toss lightly. When ready to serve, garnish with salsa, sour cream and tortilla chips.

Serves 8.

Side Dishes

Frijoles
(Pinto Beans)

1 lb. dried PINTO BEANS, sorted and rinsed
WATER
1 lg. ONION, chopped
2 cloves GARLIC, minced
1/4 tsp. OREGANO
SALT and PEPPER, to taste

Place beans in a large pot and add water to cover. Soak beans overnight. (For quicker use, bring to boil for five minutes, remove from heat and let soak, covered for one hour.) Drain beans. Cover with fresh water and add onion, garlic, oregano and pepper. Bring to a boil, reduce heat and simmer, covered, until beans are tender (approximately 3 hours). Add water as necessary. To avoid making the beans too tough, season with salt shortly before beans have reached desired tenderness.

Serves 6.

Spanish Rice

1 1/2 cups uncooked WHITE RICE
2 1/2 Tbsp. MARGARINE
1 ONION, chopped
1 sm. GREEN BELL PEPPER, diced
2 cloves GARLIC, minced
1 can (8 oz.) TOMATO SAUCE
3 cups WATER
1/2 tsp. OREGANO
1/4 tsp. CHILI POWDER
SALT to taste

In large nonstick frying pan, brown rice in margarine. Add onion, bell pepper and garlic. Sauté for two minutes. Add tomato sauce, water and seasonings. Bring to a boil, lower heat to simmer, cover and cook until rice is tender and all moisture is absorbed.

Serves 6.

Calabacitas

(Squash)

6 ZUCCHINI SQUASH, sliced
1 ONION, chopped
2 cloves GARLIC, minced
1 lg. TOMATO, chopped
1 can (15 oz.) CORN
1 can (16 oz.) STEWED TOMATOES,
    chopped
SALT to taste
3/4 cup shredded JACK CHEESE

Preheat oven to 350°. Place all ingredients, except cheese, into casserole dish. Cover and bake until vegetables are tender, approximately 20 minutes (or microwave on HIGH for approximately 10 minutes). Remove from heat and sprinkle with cheese. Serve hot.

Serves 8.

Calabicitas con Limas

(Squash with Lima Beans)

2 lbs. SUMMER SQUASH, diced
1 Tbsp. MARGARINE
1/2 ONION, diced
2 TOMATOES, diced
1 can (4 oz.) diced GREEN CHILES
2 cups cooked LIMA BEANS
1/4 tsp. GARLIC POWDER
SALT and PEPPER to taste

Boil squash until tender and drain. In a large nonstick skillet, sauté onion in margarine until tender. Add squash, tomatoes, chiles, lima beans and seasonings. Mix well. Cover and simmer for five minutes.

Serves 6.

Santa Fe Mashed Potatoes

4 RUSSET POTATOES
2 Tbsp. OLIVE OIL
2 cloves GARLIC, minced
1 RED ONION, chopped
1 can (4 oz.) diced GREEN CHILES
1/2 cup SOUR CREAM
1/4 cup fresh CILANTRO, chopped
SALT and PEPPER to taste

Wash and cut potatoes into 2-inch pieces. Place in pot and cover with cold water. Boil for 20 minutes or until tender. While potatoes are cooking, sauté garlic and onion in olive oil in a skillet. When onion is tender add green chiles. Drain and mash potatoes. Stir in sour cream, onion mixture and cilantro. Season with salt and pepper and mix well.

Serves 4.

Camotes en Jarabe
(Sweet Potatoes in Syrup)

4 medium SWEET POTATOES
1 cup BROWN SUGAR
2 Tbsp. MARGARINE
1 can (17 oz.) PINEAPPLE chunks
1 1/2 cups WATER
2 Tbsp. grated ORANGE PEEL
1 tsp. CINNAMON
1/2 tsp. NUTMEG

Wash and peel potatoes and cut into 2-inch pieces. In a large saucepan mix brown sugar, margarine, pineapple, water, orange peel, cinnamon and nutmeg. Bring to a boil. Reduce heat and simmer until thick and syrup has reduced. Add sweet potatoes, cover, and continue to simmer for 30 minutes or until tender. Serve warm or chilled.

Serves 6-8.

South of the Border Pasta

8 oz. PASTA
1 pkg. (8 oz.) CREAM CHEESE
2 Tbsp. diced JALAPEÑO
1/2 cup chopped fresh CILANTRO
1/2 tsp. GARLIC SALT

Cook pasta according to package directions. In a saucepan combine cream cheese, jalapeños, cilantro and garlic salt. Gently warm over low heat, stirring to blend ingredients. In a large bowl, pour cream cheese sauce over pasta and stir to mix thoroughly. Serve warm.

Serves 4.

Chile Rice Olé

Try this recipe as an alternative to Spanish rice.

4 cups cooked RICE
1/2 ONION, chopped
1/2 cup diced RED BELL PEPPER
1 can (7 oz.) diced GREEN CHILES
2 cups SOUR CREAM
1 cup shredded COLBY JACK CHEESE

Combine all ingredients and pour into a lightly oiled baking dish. Bake in oven at 350° for 30 minutes.

Serves 4.

Chile Cornbread

1 cup CORNMEAL
1 cup FLOUR
1 Tbsp. BAKING POWDER
1 tsp. SALT
1 1/2 cups MILK
2 EGGS, slightly beaten
1 can (4 oz.) diced GREEN
    CHILES, drained
1 can (15 oz.) CORN, drained
4 Tbsp. SALSA
1 cup shredded CHEDDAR CHEESE

Mix all ingredients together in a large bowl. Pour into a nonstick 9 x 13 baking pan. Bake at 350° for 45 minutes, or until toothpick inserted in center comes out clean. Serve warm or allow to cool.

Chile Hominy

Use this recipe in place of potatoes or rice.

2 cans (15 oz. each) HOMINY
1 can (7 oz.) diced GREEN CHILES
1 can (10.75 oz.) CREAM OF MUSHROOM SOUP
1 cup SOUR CREAM
1/8 tsp. ground CUMIN
1/4 tsp. PEPPER
1 Tbsp. dried CILANTRO
1 cup shredded LONGHORN CHEESE
1 can (2 oz.) sliced BLACK OLIVES

Preheat oven to 350°. Pour hominy into a colander, rinse well with water and allow to drain. In a large bowl combine hominy, chiles, soup, sour cream, seasonings and 1/2 cup cheese. Mix well and pour into a lightly oiled casserole dish. Sprinkle remaining cheese and olives on top and bake for 45 minutes.

Serves 8.

Papas Verde
(Green Potatoes)

1 ONION, chopped
2 JALAPEÑOS, seeded and diced
1 clove GARLIC, minced
1 Tbsp. VEGETABLE OIL
2 lbs. POTATOES, cut into 1-inch cubes
2 cans (8 oz. each) TOMATO SAUCE
1 can (7 oz.) diced GREEN CHILES
2 Tbsp. CORNSTARCH
1/4 cup WATER

In a large skillet, sauté onion, jalapeños and garlic in vegetable oil. Add potatoes and continue to cook. When potatoes begin to brown, add tomato sauce and green chiles. Cover and simmer for 30 minutes. In a small bowl dissolve cornstarch in 1/4 cup water and stir into potato mixture to thicken sauce. Serve with warm tortillas.

Serves 6.

Papas Colorado
(Red Potatoes)

2 lbs. POTATOES, cut into 1-inch cubes
1/2 RED BELL PEPPER, diced
3 Tbsp. chopped fresh CILANTRO
1 tsp. GARLIC SALT
4 Tbsp. SALSA
1/2 Tbsp. crushed RED PEPPER FLAKES

Boil potatoes until tender and drain thoroughly. Return potatoes to cooking pot and add remaining ingredients. Gently stir to coat potatoes. Serve hot.

Serves 6.

Refried Anasazi Beans

1 lb. dried ANASAZI® BEANS
2 Tbsp. VEGETABLE OIL
1/4 cup finely chopped ONION
1/4 cup finely chopped GREEN BELL PEPPER
1 clove GARLIC, crushed
1 tsp. CHILI POWDER

Place beans in a large kettle, add 6 cups water and cook, at a gentle boil, 1 1/2 hours or until beans are tender. Drain beans, reserving liquid. Sauté onion, green pepper and garlic. Mash beans together with sautéed mixture and chili powder, adding reserved bean liquid a little at a time, until bean mixture is smooth. This recipe freezes well.

Serves 6-8

Black Beans & Corn

This delicious side dish is great served warm and also tastes wonderful as a chilled salad accompaniment!

2 cans (15 oz. each) BLACK BEANS, drained and rinsed
2 cans (15 oz. each) CORN, drained
1 can (15 oz.) MEXICAN STYLE STEWED TOMATOES
1 RED ONION, chopped
1 can (4 oz.) sliced BLACK OLIVES
1 bunch GREEN ONIONS, chopped
1/2 bunch CILANTRO, chopped
1/2 tsp. CHILI POWDER
1/2 tsp. GARLIC SALT
1/4 tsp. ground CUMIN
1/4 tsp. PEPPER

Combine all ingredients in a large saucepan and heat on medium heat until warmed through.

Serves 8.

Spicy Stuffed Potatoes

3 lg. RUSSET POTATOES
1/2 cup COTTAGE CHEESE
1/2 cup SOUR CREAM
1 can (4 oz.) diced GREEN CHILES
1 Tbsp. diced JALAPEÑOS
1/2 tsp. GARLIC SALT
1/2 bunch fresh CILANTRO, chopped
1/2 cup shredded LONGHORN CHEESE
PAPRIKA

Bake potatoes and allow to cool until easy to handle. Slice in half lengthwise and scoop out centers, leaving 1/2-inch rim; and set shells aside. Mash potato centers and combine with cottage cheese and sour cream, blending thoroughly. Stir in green chiles, jalapeños, garlic salt and cilantro. Fill potato skins with mixture, sprinkle with cheese and paprika and place in 350° oven for 10-15 minutes, or until crispy on top.

Serves 6.

Mexican Casserole

4 cups cooked PINTO BEANS
1 can (15 oz.) STEWED TOMATOES, chopped
1/2 GREEN BELL PEPPER, chopped
1/2 ONION, chopped
1 can (2 oz.) sliced BLACK OLIVES
1 cup shredded JACK CHEESE
1/2 tsp. GARLIC SALT
1 tsp. CHILI POWDER
1/4 tsp. ground CUMIN

Combine all ingredients and turn into a baking dish. Bake in a 350° oven for 1 hour.

Serves 8.

Mexican-Style Macaroni

This is a great way to spice up your macaroni and cheese!

1 Tbsp. VEGETABLE OIL
1/2 ONION, chopped
3 Tbsp. diced GREEN CHILES
1 Tbsp. diced JALAPEÑOS
1 Tbsp. FLOUR
1 tsp. GARLIC SALT
1 tsp. CHILI POWDER

1/4 tsp. ground CUMIN
1 pkg. (8 oz.) ELBOW
   MACARONI
3 1/2 cups MILK
1/2 cup COTTAGE CHEESE
1 cup shredded CHEDDAR
   CHEESE

In a large skillet, sauté onion in oil. Add green chiles and jalapeños and stir in flour, garlic salt, chili powder and cumin. Add macaroni and milk. Cover and bring to a boil. Reduce heat and simmer 15 minutes or until macaroni is tender, stirring occasionally. Add cottage cheese and cheddar cheese and heat until cheese melts.

Serves 6.

Fiesta Hominy

Hominy is dried white or yellow corn kernels from which the hull and germ have been removed. This colorful side dish is a great alternative to rice or potatoes.

2 Tbsp. FLOUR
2 Tbsp. OIL
1/3 cup diced ONION
1/2 GREEN BELL
   PEPPER, diced
1 TOMATO, sliced

1 can (29 oz.) HOMINY, drained
   and rinsed
2 cups WATER
1/2 tsp. GARLIC SALT
1/4 tsp. OREGANO
dash PEPPER

Brown flour in oil. Add onion and sauté. Add bell pepper and tomato and stir over medium heat. Stir in hominy, water and seasonings. Cover and simmer for 15 minutes over medium heat, stirring occasionally.

Serves 6.

Arroz de Mexico

(Mexican Rice)

2 Tbsp. MARGARINE
2 cups uncooked RICE
3 cups VEGETABLE BROTH
1/2 ONION, diced
1/2 GREEN BELL PEPPER, diced
1 cup frozen PEAS
1 can (15 oz.) MEXICAN STYLE STEWED TOMATOES
1 CARROT, grated
1/2 tsp. GARLIC SALT
1/4 tsp. ground CUMIN

Heat oil in a large skillet and sauté rice until golden. Add 1/2 cup broth, onion and bell pepper and sauté for 2 more minutes. Stir in remaining broth and balance of ingredients. Bring to a boil, reduce heat, cover and simmer for 20 minutes or until broth is absorbed.

Serves 8.

Baked Hominy

1 can (29 oz.) HOMINY, drained and rinsed
1 can (7 oz.) diced GREEN CHILES
1 1/2 cups SOUR CREAM
1 cup shredded CHEDDAR CHEESE
1/4 tsp. CAYENNE PEPPER

Combine all ingredients and pour into a casserole dish. Cover and bake at 350° for 20 minutes.

Serves 6.

Lemon Rice

2 cups WATER
1/4 cup LEMON JUICE
1/4 cup LIME JUICE
2 Tbsp. grated LEMON RIND

1/2 tsp. GARLIC SALT
1/4 tsp. OREGANO
1 cup WHITE RICE, uncooked
fresh CILANTRO, to taste

In a saucepan, combine water, lemon and lime juices, lemon rind, garlic salt and oregano and bring to a boil. Reduce heat and stir in rice. Cover and simmer for 30 minutes or until all liquid has been absorbed. Just before serving, while still hot, add chopped cilantro and toss gently.

Serves 4.

Tofu Chili Colorado

A great accompaniment to tacos and burritos. This is also a great vegetarian filling for tortillas.

1 cake (12 oz.) firm TOFU, cut into cubes
2 Tbsp. VEGETABLE OIL
2 Tbsp. FLOUR
1 RED BELL PEPPER, seeded and cut into large chunks
1 ONION, quartered
2 POTATOES, cut into large chunks
3 cups WATER
3 Tbsp. CHILI POWDER
1/2 tsp. GARLIC SALT
1/4 tsp. ground CUMIN

In a large pot, brown tofu in oil. Sprinkle and stir in flour. Add pepper, onion and potatoes. Add water and bring to a boil. Reduce heat, stir in seasonings, cover and simmer 2 hours.

Serves 6.

Main Dishes

Green Chile Sauce

This basic sauce can be used over many traditional Mexican dishes such as enchiladas, burros, tostadas and huevos rancheros. Green chile sauce is more perishable than red and should be made fresh.

1 lb. TOMATILLOS
8 fresh, roasted and peeled NEW MEXICO
GREEN CHILES, chopped
1 lg. ONION, chopped
1-2 cloves GARLIC, chopped
2 cups VEGETABLE BROTH
1/2 tsp. SALT
1/4 tsp. ground CUMIN
1/4 tsp. OREGANO

Husk and wash tomatillos. Slice into wedges. In a large saucepan combine tomatillos, chiles, onion, garlic, broth and seasonings. Bring to a boil, reduce heat and simmer for 20 minutes. Pour into blender and pulse to desired consistency.

Makes approximately 4 cups.

Green Salsa Sauce

1 ONION, chopped
1/2 cup CILANTRO
1 Tbsp. BASIL
1 Tbsp. DILL
1 Tbsp. LEMON JUICE

1/4 tsp. ground CUMIN
1 clove GARLIC
3/4 cup OLIVE OIL
dash BLACK PEPPER
1 Tbsp. TAMARI

Combine all ingredients in a blender and blend for 1 minute. Chill and serve.

Makes 1 cup.

Red Chile Sauce

This versatile sauce can be used for covering burritos, huevos rancheros, tostadas or making chile stews.

8 lg. dried RED CHILE PODS
2 cloves GARLIC
1 med. ONION, chopped
WATER
2 Tbsp. FLOUR

2 cups WATER
1 tsp. OREGANO
1/4 tsp. ground CUMIN
SALT to taste

Wash chiles, remove stems and seeds (leave seeds if you prefer a hotter sauce). Place chiles, garlic and onion in a pot and cover with water. Bring to a boil, reduce heat and cook for 45 minutes. Drain water. Place chiles, garlic, onion and flour in a blender and purée till smooth. Pour into saucepan, add 2 cups water and seasonings. Cook over medium heat, stirring constantly, until sauce is thick and bubbly.

Makes 3 cups.

Red Flash

This is an easy, quick version of a red chile sauce.

3 Tbsp. FLOUR
1/4 cup WATER
2 cups VEGETABLE BROTH
1/2 cup RED CHILE POWDER
1 tsp. GARLIC SALT
1/2 tsp. OREGANO
1/4 tsp. ground CUMIN

Mix flour and 1/4 cup water in a saucepan, stirring until smooth. Add 2 cups broth, chile powder, garlic salt, oregano and cumin and cook over medium heat, stirring constantly, for 5 minutes or until thick and bubbly.

Makes 2 cups.

Bean Tostadas

12 CORN TORTILLAS
VEGETABLE OIL
1 can (15 oz.) VEGETARIAN REFRIED BEANS
1/2 head LETTUCE, shredded
1 cup shredded LONGHORN CHEESE
1 sm. ONION, diced
2 TOMATOES, diced
SOUR CREAM
SALSA

In a skillet, fry tortillas in hot oil until crisp (approximately 1 minute per side). Drain on paper towels. Warm beans and spread on tortillas. Layer with lettuce, cheese, onion and tomatoes. Serve with sour cream and salsa.

Serves 6.

Tofu Tostadas

1 cake (8 oz.) firm TOFU, diced
2 Tbsp. VEGETABLE OIL
1 can (4 oz.) diced GREEN CHILES
1/2 tsp. GARLIC SALT
12 TOSTADA SHELLS
1 can (15 oz.) VEGETARIAN REFRIED BEANS
1/2 head LETTUCE, shredded
1 cup shredded LONGHORN CHEESE
2 TOMATOES, diced
SOUR CREAM
SALSA

In a skillet, fry tofu until golden brown. Add green chiles and garlic salt and continue to cook for 2 minutes.   Warm beans and spread on tostada shells. Add tofu mixture and layer lettuce, cheese and tomatoes. Serve with sour cream and salsa.

Serves 6.

Guacamole Tostadas

12 CORN TORTILLAS
VEGETABLE OIL
1 cup GUACAMOLE (see page 18)
1/2 head LETTUCE, shredded
1 cup shredded JACK CHEESE

2 TOMATOES, diced
3 GREEN ONIONS, diced
SOUR CREAM
SALSA

In a skillet, fry tortillas in hot oil until crisp. Drain on paper towels. Spread guacamole on tortillas. Layer with lettuce, cheese, tomatoes, onions and a dollop of sour cream. Add salsa to taste.

Serves 6.

Mexican Pizza

1 can (15 oz.) VEGETARIAN REFRIED BEANS
1 ONION, finely diced
1/2 tsp. GARLIC SALT
1/2 tsp. OREGANO
1/4 tsp. ground CUMIN
4 (10-inch) FLOUR TORTILLAS
1 can (4 oz.) diced GREEN CHILES, drained
1 cup shredded JACK CHEESE
1 cup shredded CHEDDAR CHEESE
2 TOMATOES, chopped
1 bunch GREEN ONIONS, chopped
1 GREEN BELL PEPPER, diced
1 can (4 oz.) sliced BLACK OLIVES
SALSA

Heat beans and onion in a skillet. Stir in seasonings. Slightly crisp tortillas in hot oven. Spread beans on tortillas and add green chiles, cheese, tomatoes, green onions, bell pepper and olives. Place under broiler until cheese melts. Serve with salsa.

Serves 4.

Potato Enchiladas

2 cups diced cooked POTATOES
2 cups shredded JACK CHEESE
2 diced JALAPEÑOS
2 Tbsp. LIME JUICE
3 chopped GREEN ONIONS
1/4 cup chopped CILANTRO
1/2 tsp. SALT
3/4 cup SOUR CREAM

8 CORN TORTILLAS
3 cups GREEN CHILE
     SAUCE (see page 54)
1/2 cup shredded CHEDDAR
     CHEESE
1 can (2 oz.) sliced BLACK
     OLIVES

Combine first eight ingredients in a large bowl. Soften tortillas in heated chile sauce. Spoon equal amounts of potato mixture onto tortillas and roll up. Place enchiladas seam-side down in a shallow baking dish. Top with remaining sauce and sprinkle with cheddar cheese. Garnish with olives and bake in a preheated 325° oven for 15 minutes.

Serves 4.

Cheese Enchiladas

4 cups RED CHILE SAUCE (see page 55)
12 CORN TORTILLAS
1 1/2 cups shredded COLBY JACK CHEESE
1 ONION, chopped
3 GREEN ONIONS, sliced
1 TOMATO, chopped
SOUR CREAM

Preheat oven to 325°. Dip each tortilla into chile sauce and transfer to platter. Place equal amounts of cheese on each tortilla and sprinkle with chopped onion. Roll up and place seam-side down in a shallow baking dish. Top with remaining sauce and sprinkle with cheese. Bake for 25 minutes. To serve, garnish with green onions, tomatoes and dollops of sour cream.

Serves 6.

Mushroom Enchiladas

8 oz. fresh MUSHROOMS
1 lg. ONION, finely chopped
2 Tbsp. MARGARINE
8 CORN TORTILLAS
4 cups RED CHILE SAUCE (see page 55)

2 cups shredded JACK CHEESE
3 GREEN ONIONS, diced
1 can (2 oz.) sliced BLACK OLIVES
SOUR CREAM

Slice and sauté mushrooms and onion in margarine. Set aside. Soften tortillas in heated chile sauce. Spoon mushrooms onto each tortilla, sprinkle with cheese and roll up; place seam-side down in a shallow baking dish. Top with remaining sauce and sprinkle with cheese. Bake in a preheated 325° oven for 15 minutes. Garnish with green onions, olives and sour cream.

Serves 4.

Green Chile Enchilada Casserole

12 CORN TORTILLAS
1 can (10.75 oz.) CREAM OF MUSHROOM SOUP
1 cup WATER
1 can (7 oz.) diced GREEN CHILES
1 ONION, finely chopped

1 1/2 cups shredded COLBY JACK CHEESE
1 can (2 oz.) sliced BLACK OLIVES
2 GREEN ONIONS, chopped
1 TOMATO, chopped

Preheat oven to 325°. Cut tortillas into 1-inch strips and set aside. Thoroughly combine soup, water, green chiles and onion. Line bottom of 9 x 13 baking dish with half of tortilla strips. Spread soup mixture over the top. Sprinkle with half of the cheese. Layer remaining tortilla strips and soup mixture and top with balance of cheese. Bake uncovered for one hour. Garnish with olives, green onions and tomato.

Serves 6.

Sonoran Enchiladas

These enchiladas differ from traditional enchiladas in that they are stacked instead of rolled.

2 cups RED CHILE SAUCE (see page 55)
12 CORN TORTILLAS
1 1/2 cups shredded LONGHORN CHEESE
1 ONION, chopped
LETTUCE, shredded
2 TOMATOES, chopped
4 GREEN ONIONS, chopped
SOUR CREAM
SALSA

Heat chile sauce thoroughly in a saucepan. Dip tortilla in sauce and lay flat on oven-proof platter or cookie sheet. Ladle 1 tablespoon of sauce over the tortilla and sprinkle with cheese and chopped onion. Repeat this process to form a stack of three for each serving. Bake in 350° oven for 10 minutes. Remove to serving dish and garnish with lettuce, tomato and green onions. Serve with sour cream and salsa.

Serves 6.

Guacamole Tacos

8 TACO SHELLS
2 cups GUACAMOLE (see page 18)
1/2 head LETTUCE, shredded
2 TOMATOES, chopped

1 can (2 oz.) sliced BLACK OLIVES
1 cup shredded CHEDDAR CHEESE

Fill each taco shell with guacamole, lettuce, tomato, olives and cheese. Serve with **SALSA.**

Serves 4.

Low Fat Bean Tacos

1 can (15 oz.) FAT FREE REFRIED BEANS
1 can (15 oz.) BLACK BEANS, drained
1 ONION, finely chopped
1 can (4 oz.) diced GREEN CHILES, drained
1/2 tsp. CHILI POWDER
1/4 tsp. GARLIC POWDER
12 TACO SHELLS
1 cup shredded LOW FAT CHEDDAR CHEESE
1/2 head LETTUCE, shredded
2 TOMATOES, chopped
SALSA

In a saucepan, combine beans, onion, chiles and seasonings. Heat thoroughly. Spoon bean mixture into taco shells. Sprinkle cheese, add lettuce and tomatoes. Top with salsa.

Serves 6.

No Fat Taco Shells

12 CORN TORTILLAS

Drape tortillas over individual rungs on oven rack. Bake at 400° until crisp (approximately 5 minutes). Carefully remove the taco shells and allow to cool.

Bean Burros

1 can (15 oz.) VEGETARIAN REFRIED BEANS
4 (12-inch) FLOUR TORTILLAS
1/2 ONION, finely chopped
1 cup shredded CHEDDAR CHEESE

Heat beans and spoon into warmed tortillas. Sprinkle with onions and cheese and roll up burro-style. Serve with **shredded LETTUCE, chopped TOMATO,** and **SALSA.**

Variation: For **Enchilada-style Bean Burros,** place burro on oven-proof platter and ladle *Red Chile Sauce* (see page 55) over the top. Sprinkle with cheese and place under broiler for 1 minute.

Serves 4.

Potato & Chile Burro

2 cups cooked, cubed POTATOES
1 Tbsp. VEGETABLE OIL
1 can (4 oz.) diced GREEN CHILES
1 can (10.75 oz.) CREAM OF MUSHROOM SOUP
1/2 cup WATER
3 GREEN ONIONS, sliced
4 (12-inch) FLOUR TORTILLAS
1 cup shredded JACK CHEESE

Sauté potatoes in oil until browned. Add chiles, soup, water and green onions. Heat thoroughly and spoon into warmed flour tortillas. Sprinkle with cheese and roll burro-style. Serve with **shredded LETTUCE, chopped TOMATOES, SOUR CREAM** and **SALSA.**

Serves 4.

Red Chile Burros

3 cups diced POTATOES
2 Tbsp. VEGETABLE OIL
1 ONION, chopped
2 cloves GARLIC, minced
1/4 tsp. OREGANO
1 cup RED CHILE SAUCE (see page 55)
2 cups cooked PINTO BEANS
6 (12-inch) FLOUR TORTILLAS
1 1/2 cups shredded LONGHORN CHEESE
shredded LETTUCE
chopped TOMATOES
SOUR CREAM
SALSA

Sauté potatoes in oil until browned. Add onion, garlic, oregano, chile sauce and pinto beans. Simmer for 10 minutes. Spoon potato mixture on flour tortillas, sprinkle with cheese and roll burro-style. Garnish with lettuce, tomatoes, sour cream and salsa.

Serves 6.

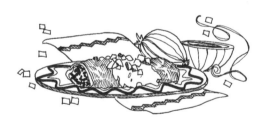

Veggie Burros

2 Tbsp. VEGETABLE OIL
1 ONION, chopped
1 GREEN BELL PEPPER, chopped
1 ZUCCHINI, sliced
1 cup BROCCOLI florets
2 CARROTS, sliced
1 can (4 oz.) diced GREEN CHILES
1/2 tsp. GARLIC SALT
1/8 tsp. ground CUMIN
1/8 tsp. OREGANO
6 (12-inch) FLOUR TORTILLAS
1/2 head LETTUCE, shredded
1 TOMATO, chopped
SALSA
SOUR CREAM
GUACAMOLE (see page 18)

Heat oil in a large skillet and sauté onion, bell pepper, zucchini, broccoli and carrots. When vegetables are tender, add chiles and seasonings. Stir and simmer for 5 minutes. Spoon into warmed flour tortillas and roll burro-style. Garnish with lettuce, tomato, salsa, sour cream and guacamole.

Serves 6.

Variation: For **Enchilada Style,** place burro on oven-proof platter and ladle *Red Chile Sauce* (see page 55) over top. Sprinkle with **shredded CHEESE** and place under broiler for 1 minute.

Mexican Stuffed Peppers

8 lg. GREEN or RED BELL PEPPERS
1 1/2 cups cooked RICE
1 TOMATO, finely diced
2 GREEN ONIONS, finely chopped
1 can (4 oz.) diced GREEN CHILES
1 1/2 cups shredded JACK CHEESE
1/2 tsp. GARLIC SALT
1/4 tsp. PEPPER
1/2 tsp. OREGANO
3 Tbsp. SALSA
1 EGG , slightly beaten
1 can (8 oz.) TOMATO SAUCE

Try to choose block-shaped bell peppers so they will stand in a baking dish. Wash and seed bell peppers. Set in baking dish. In a large bowl, combine cooked rice, tomato, onions, green chiles, cheese, seasonings, salsa and egg. Blend well. Fill each pepper with rice mixture. Pour tomato sauce over peppers and bake in a pre-heated 350° oven for 45 minutes.

Serves 8.

Fajita Marinade

1/2 cup WATER
1/4 cup LEMON JUICE
2 cloves GARLIC, crushed
1 Tbsp. WORCESTERSHIRE SAUCE
1/2 tsp. OREGANO
1/2 tsp. ground CUMIN
2 tsp. BROWN SUGAR
dash of TABASCO®
1/8 tsp. LIQUID SMOKE

Place all ingredients in a glass bowl and blend well. Marinate tofu or vegetables, in the refrigerator, for at least one hour before cooking.

Vegetable Fajitas

1 ONION, sliced into wedges
1 GREEN BELL PEPPER, sliced
1 RED BELL PEPPER, sliced
1 ZUCCHINI, sliced
1 1/2 cups CAULIFLOWER florets
1 1/2 cups BROCCOLI florets
2 CARROTS, sliced
FAJITA MARINADE (see above)
2 Tbsp. VEGETABLE OIL

Marinate vegetables in fajita marinade for 1 hour in the refrigerator. In a large skillet, heat oil and sauté vegetables until tender. Serve with warmed **FLOUR TORTILLAS,** and top with **shredded LETTUCE, chopped TOMATOES, SOUR CREAM, SALSA,** *Guacamole* (see page 18), *Pico de Gallo* (see page 19) and *Frijoles* (see page 42).

Serves 6.

Tofu Fajitas

1 cake (12 oz.) firm TOFU, sliced
FAJITA MARINADE (see page 66)
1 Tbsp. VEGETABLE OIL
1 GREEN BELL PEPPER, cut into strips
1 ONION, cut into wedges
1 TOMATO, cut into wedges

Place tofu in shallow baking dish or a locking plastic bag. Pour marinade over tofu slices and refrigerate for 1-2 hours. In hot nonstick skillet, sauté marinated tofu in oil. Add vegetables and continue cooking until tender. Serve with warmed **FLOUR** or **CORN TORTILLAS.** Accompany with plenty of shredded **LETTUCE,** chopped **TOMATOES, SOUR CREAM, SALSA,** *Pico de Gallo* (see page 19), *Guacamole* (see page 18), and *Frijoles* (see page 42).

Tamale Pie

1 cup CORNMEAL
1 EGG
1 1/2 cups MILK
1 Tbsp. CHILI POWDER
1/2 tsp. GARLIC SALT
1/4 tsp. ground CUMIN
1/4 tsp. CAYENNE PEPPER
1 can (15 oz.) WHOLE KERNEL CORN, drained
1 can (15 oz.) STEWED TOMATOES, cut up
1 can (4 oz.) diced GREEN CHILES, drained
4 GREEN ONIONS, chopped
1 can (4 oz.) sliced BLACK OLIVES
1 1/2 cups shredded LONGHORN CHEESE

In a large bowl, combine cornmeal, egg and milk. Add seasonings, corn, tomatoes, green chiles, green onion, olives and 1/2 cup cheese. Mix thoroughly and pour into a lightly oiled casserole dish. Sprinkle remaining cup of cheese over the top. Cover and bake at 325° for 45 minutes.

Serves 6-8.

Green Chile Stew

This satisfying stew is a great way to warm up on a cold winter day.

1 ONION, chopped
1 GREEN or RED BELL PEPPER, chopped
1 clove GARLIC, crushed
2 Tbsp. VEGETABLE OIL
3 CARROTS, sliced
3 POTATOES, cubed
1 can (15 oz.) STEWED TOMATOES, drained
2 cans (15 oz. each) PINTO BEANS
1 can (7 oz.) diced GREEN CHILES
2 cups VEGETABLE BROTH
2 cups GREEN CHILE SAUCE (see page 54)
SALT and PEPPER to taste

In large pot, sauté onion, pepper and garlic in oil. Add remaining ingredients and bring to a boil. Reduce heat, cover and simmer for 1 hour. Serve with warmed **FLOUR TORTILLAS.**

Serves 6.

Low Fat Mexican Lasagna

Sauce:
- 1 Tbsp. OLIVE OIL
- 1 GREEN BELL PEPPER, diced
- 1 ONION, chopped
- 3 cloves GARLIC, crushed
- 1 can (7 oz.) diced GREEN CHILES
- 1 jar (16 oz.) SALSA
- 1 can (16 oz.) STEWED TOMATOES, chopped
- 1 can (8 oz.) TOMATO SAUCE
- 1/2 tsp. OREGANO
- 1/2 tsp. ground CUMIN
- 1/2 tsp. PEPPER

Heat oil in a large skillet and sauté bell pepper, onion and garlic until tender. Add green chiles, salsa, tomatoes, tomato sauce and seasonings. Simmer for 20 minutes.

Cheese Filling:
- 1 carton (16 oz.) FAT FREE COTTAGE CHEESE
- 1 cup LOW FAT RICOTTA CHEESE
- 1 can (4 oz.) diced GREEN CHILES
- 2 EGG WHITES
- 1/2 tsp. OREGANO
- 1/4 cup chopped fresh CILANTRO

Combine cottage and ricotta cheeses with chiles, egg whites, oregano and cilantro.

12 CORN TORTILLAS, torn in half
1 cup shredded LOW FAT JACK CHEESE

Spoon 1/3 of the sauce into a 9 x 13 baking dish and cover with half of the tortilla pieces. Spread half of the cheese filling over top. Spoon 1/3 of tomato sauce over the cheese filling and sprinkle with 1/2 cup jack cheese. Layer remaining tortilla pieces, cheese filling and remaining sauce. Top with jack cheese. Bake at 350° for one hour. Let stand 10 minutes before serving. Garnish with fresh **TOMATOES** and **sprigs of CILANTRO**.

Serves 8-10.

Mexican Spinach Lasagna

1 ONION, chopped
1 Tbsp. OLIVE OIL
1 can (15 oz.) STEWED TOMATOES, chopped
1 can (4 oz.) diced GREEN CHILES
1 can (2 oz.) sliced BLACK OLIVES
1/2 cup SALSA
1 can (8 oz.) TOMATO SAUCE
2 Tbsp. CHILI POWDER
1/2 tsp. OREGANO
1/2 tsp. GARLIC SALT
1 cup COTTAGE CHEESE
1/2 cup SOUR CREAM
1 lb. pkg. frozen SPINACH, thawed and excess
    water squeezed out
12 CORN TORTILLAS
2 cups shredded JACK CHEESE

In a large skillet, sauté onion in oil. Stir in tomatoes, green chiles, olives, salsa, tomato sauce, and seasonings. Simmer for 20 minutes. Combine cottage cheese, sour cream and spinach together. Spoon 1/4 of the tomato sauce mixture in the bottom of a 9 x 13 baking dish. Arrange 4 tortillas over the sauce. Spread 1/3 of the cottage cheese/spinach mixture over the tortillas and sprinkle with 1/3 of the jack cheese. Repeat two more layers ending with the cheese on top. Bake for 30 minutes in a 325° oven. Allow to set for 10 minutes before serving.

Serves 8.

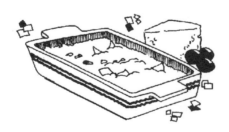

Black Bean & Brown Rice Burritos

This nutritional combination of black beans and brown rice is a valuable source of protein and is sure to become one of your favorites!

1 can (15 oz.) BLACK BEANS, drained
1 lg. ONION, finely grated
1 can (4 oz.) diced GREEN CHILES
2 Tbsp. chopped fresh CILANTRO
1 tsp. RED CHILI POWDER
8 WHOLE WHEAT FLOUR TORTILLAS
2 cups cooked BROWN RICE
1 cup shredded JACK CHEESE
1 cup SALSA

Preheat oven to 350°. In a large mixing bowl, mash beans with grated onion. Stir in chiles, cilantro and chili powder. Spread tortillas out on a counter and place equal amounts of the bean mixture on each one. Top with a 1/4 cup of cooked brown rice, and sprinkle with cheese. Fold in sides and roll tortilla to completely enclose contents. Place all eight burritos, seam-side down, in a nonstick baking pan. Pour salsa evenly over the burritos and bake at 350° for 20 minutes.

Serves 8

Green Corn Tamales

12 ears white, tender CORN (save husks)
1 cup MILK
1 1/2 Tbsp. SALT
1 cup VEGETABLE SHORTENING
1/2 cup MARGARINE
2 cups grated LONGHORN CHEESE
12 fresh ANAHEIM CHILES

Cut the ends of the corn with a sharp knife, and remove husks. Save all husks, remove corn silk and wash. Remove corn from cob with a large knife. Grind corn as finely as possible in a food processor. Add milk, salt, shortening and margarine into food processor and blend well. Add cheese and blend well. Corn mixture should have a smooth and spreadable texture. This will be the "masa" although it will be more moist and fluffier than regular masa.

Roast green chiles in 350° oven until fully roasted. Remove skins, seeds, and cut into long strips. Choose the larger corn husks, rinse them in cold water and drain.

Spoon corn mixture on wider end of corn husks. Spread thin, even layer over most of the corn husk but not the narrow end. Add strips of chiles. Fold husk sides to cover masa and chiles. Fold husk tails up. Set upright so that masa shows. Repeat until all the masa is used.

Cook tamales in a steamer or a large cooking pot. If you use a cooking pot, line pot with aluminum foil or extra corn husks. Place tamales in upright position around a crumpled ball of foil at the center of the pot to help hold tamales in place. Add 1 cup of water carefully to side of pot. Try not to get tamales wet. Let boil, cover, then cook over medium heat for 1 hour. Add 1/2 cup water every 20 minutes to keep tamales from drying out. Remove husks just before eating.

Makes 30 tamales.   Total preparation time: 2 1/2 hours.

Sloppy Jose's

1 ONION, chopped
1 GREEN BELL PEPPER, chopped
1 clove GARLIC, crushed
1 can (4 oz.) diced GREEN CHILES
2 cups cooked, or canned, PINTO BEANS
1 can (15 oz.) STEWED TOMATOES
1 can (8 oz.) TOMATO SAUCE
1/2 cup WATER
3/4 cup TEXTURIZED VEGETABLE PROTEIN (TVP)
1 Tbsp. CHILI POWDER
1/2 tsp. OREGANO
SALT and PEPPER to taste

In nonstick saucepan, sauté onion, bell pepper and garlic until vegetables are tender. Add remaining ingredients and simmer for 30 minutes. Serve over split hamburger buns, cornbread or warmed tortillas.

Serves 8.

Fiesta Tofu

1 cake (12 oz.) firm TOFU, sliced
1/2 tsp. GARLIC SALT
1/2 tsp. ground CUMIN
PEPPER to taste
1 Tbsp. VEGETABLE OIL
1 can (4 oz.) diced GREEN CHILES
1 cup WHOLE KERNEL CORN
1 can (15 oz.) BLACK BEANS, drained and rinsed
1 cup SALSA
fresh CILANTRO

Season sliced tofu with garlic salt, cumin and pepper. Sauté in oil and brown on both sides in a nonstick skillet. Add green chiles, corn, black beans and salsa. Cover and simmer for 15 minutes. Garnish with fresh cilantro. Serve with rice.

Serves 4.

Green Chile Pie

1 can (7 oz.) diced GREEN CHILES, drained
3 GREEN ONIONS, sliced
1 1/2 cups shredded JACK CHEESE
1 1/2 cups shredded LONGHORN CHEESE
1 cup BISCUIT MIX
2 cups MILK
4 EGGS

Preheat oven to 425°. Spread chiles, onions and shredded cheeses in a lightly oiled deep pie plate. Combine remaining ingredients and beat until smooth. Pour over chiles, onions and cheese. Bake for 30 minutes. Allow to set for 10 minutes before slicing.

Serves 6.

Oven Omelet

8 EGGS
1 cup MILK
1/2 tsp. SALT
dash TABASCO®
1/4 cup chopped CILANTRO
2 GREEN ONIONS, chopped
1 can (7 oz.) diced GREEN CHILES
1 can (2 oz.) sliced BLACK OLIVES
1 TOMATO, diced
2 cups shredded CHEDDAR CHEESE

Preheat oven to 350°. In a large bowl, beat eggs, milk, salt and Tabasco. Stir in cilantro, green onions, green chiles, olives and tomato. Sprinkle cheese in a lightly greased 1 1/2-quart casserole dish. Pour egg mixture over the top of the cheese and bake for 45 minutes. Let stand for 5 minutes before slicing.

Serves 6-8.

For a hotter, spicier dish, substitute diced jalapeños for the green chiles.

Desserts

Capirotada

(Bread Pudding)

1 cup RAISINS
1 cup ORANGE JUICE
1/2 tsp. CINNAMON
1/2 tsp. ALLSPICE
1/2 tsp. grated ORANGE PEEL
3/4 cup BROWN SUGAR

1/2 tsp. VANILLA
10 slices BREAD
1 APPLE, peeled, cored & diced
1/2 cup unsalted PEANUTS
2 cups shredded CHEDDAR
    CHEESE

Combine raisins, orange juice, cinnamon, allspice, orange peel, brown sugar and vanilla in a saucepan and bring to a boil, stirring constantly. Toast bread and cut into cubes. Place bread cubes in a large bowl and toss with raisin mixture. Add apples, peanuts and 1 1/2 cups of grated cheese and mix together. Turn into a lightly oiled baking dish and sprinkle with remaining cheese. Bake in a preheated 375° oven for 15 minutes. Serve warm with maple or brown sugar syrup.

Serves 10.

Gelatina de Yogurt con Fresas

(Yogurt-Strawberry Gelatin)

1 pkg. (6 oz.) STRAWBERRY GELATIN
2 cups boiling WATER
2 cups STRAWBERRY YOGURT
2 cups sliced STRAWBERRIES

Dissolve gelatin in boiling water. Allow to cool for 10 minutes. Stir in yogurt and strawberries. Pour into decorative mold. Refrigerate for at least 4 hours. Unmold and serve.

Serves 8.

Holiday Capirotada

*Traditionally served during the holiday season, the aroma of
this dish makes the whole house come alive.*

8 slices BREAD, toasted
4 EGGS, beaten
1/4 cup MILK
1/4 BROWN SUGAR
1 tsp. NUTMEG
1 tsp. CINNAMON
3/4 cup slivered ALMONDS
3/4 cup PEANUTS
1/2 cup RAISINS
1 APPLE, peeled, cored and thinly sliced
1 cup shredded JACK CHEESE

Preheat oven to 350°. Lightly oil a square baking pan. Lay 4
slices of toasted bread in bottom of pan. Combine eggs, milk,
brown sugar, nutmeg and cinnamon and mix thoroughly. Combine
almonds, peanuts, raisins, and apple and sprinkle half of this
mixture over the bread. Sprinkle with half of the cheese. Pour half
of the egg mixture on top. Add another layer of bread and repeat
the layer of nuts and fruit, adding cheese on top. Pour the rest of
the egg mixture over all. Bake for 30 minutes. Serve warm with
Brown Sugar-Cinnamon Syrup.

Serves 10.

Brown Sugar-Cinnamon Syrup

2 cups BROWN SUGAR
2 cups WATER
1 CINNAMON STICK

Combine ingredients in a medium saucepan. Bring to a boil.
Reduce heat and simmer for 15 minutes or until syrup is slightly
thickened. Remove cinnamon stick.

Meringues de Chocolate
(Chocolate Meringues)

Meringues are placed in the oven to dry rather than bake. It is important not to remove them before they have completely cooled inside the oven.

4 EGG WHITES　　　　　　　　**2 Tbsp. COCOA**
1 cup SUGAR　　　　　　　　　**1/2 tsp. VANILLA**

Preheat oven to 225°. Line a cookie sheet with parchment paper. Beat egg whites until stiff. Add sugar a little at a time, continuing to beat until glossy. Dissolve cocoa in a small amount of water and add vanilla. Fold into egg whites. Drop by teaspoonfuls onto cookie sheet, leaving 1-inch between meringues. Place in oven for 1 hour, or until firm to the touch. Cool in oven before removing.

Makes 12 meringues.

Meringues de Almendra
(Almond Meringues)

4 EGG WHITES　　　　　　　　**1 cup SUGAR**
1/8 tsp. CREAM OF TARTAR　　**1 tsp. ALMOND EXTRACT**

Preheat oven to 225°. Line a cookie sheet with parchment paper. Beat egg whites until frothy. Add cream of tartar and almond extract and continue beating. Add sugar, 1 teaspoon at a time until egg whites are stiff and glossy. Drop by teaspoonfuls onto cookie sheet, leaving 1 inch between meringues. Place in oven for 1 hour, or until meringues are firm to the touch. Leave in oven to cool completely. Meringues can be stored, tightly covered, until ready to use.

Makes 12 meringues.

Flan

(Custard)

A traditional, popular Mexican dessert.

3 EGGS, slightly beaten
1/4 tsp. SALT
1 can (14 oz.) SWEETENED CONDENSED MILK
1 1/2 cups MILK
1/2 Tbsp. VANILLA
NUTMEG

In a bowl combine eggs, salt and sweetened condensed milk. Add milk slowly, stirring constantly. Add vanilla and blend well. Preheat oven to 350°. Pour custard into 6 custard dishes. Sprinkle each with nutmeg. Place custard cups in baking pan, add hot water to the pan 2/3 of the way up the sides of the custard cups. Bake for 30-35 minutes. To test for doneness, knife should come out clean when inserted into center. Refrigerate for several hours. The longer it is chilled, the firmer it becomes. To serve, top with *Flan Sauce*.

Serves 6.

Flan Sauce

6 Tbsp. BROWN SUGAR
1/2 cup WATER
1/2 tsp. CINNAMON

In a saucepan dissolve sugar by adding water slowly. Add cinnamon. Heat until smooth, clear syrup forms. Serve over flan.

Pastel de Piña

(Pineapple Cake)

2 cups SUGAR
2 cups FLOUR
2 tsp. BAKING SODA
2 EGGS
1 can (20 oz.) crushed PINEAPPLE, undrained
1 tsp. VANILLA

Preheat oven to 325°. Lightly oil a 9 x 13 baking dish. Combine all ingredients in mixing bowl and blend thoroughly. Pour into baking dish and bake for 35-40 minutes, or until tester comes out clean. Top immediately with *Cream Cheese Icing.*

Serves 12.

Cream Cheese Icing

2 cups sifted POWDERED SUGAR
1 pkg. (8 oz.) CREAM CHEESE, room temperature
2 Tbsp. MILK

Blend all ingredients until smooth. Spread on pineapple cake.

Sweet Tortilla Roll-ups

1/2 cup RICOTTA CHEESE
3 Tbsp. SUGAR
2 tsp. CINNAMON
1/4 tsp. VANILLA
4 (10-inch) FLOUR TORTILLAS

Set oven to broil. In a mixing bowl blend ricotta cheese, sugar, cinnamon and vanilla. Spread about 2 tablespoons of ricotta down center of each tortilla. Fold ends of each tortilla in and roll up like a burrito. Place on cookie sheet and broil for approximately 1 minute. Serve warm.

Serves 4.

Pastel Coctel de Fruta
(Fruit Cocktail Cake)

2 cups FLOUR
1 1/2 cups SUGAR
2 tsp. BAKING SODA
1 tsp. SALT
1 CAN (28 OZ.) FRUIT COCKTAIL, undrained
1/2 cup RAISINS
2 EGGS
2 tsp. VANILLA
3/4 cup POWDERED SUGAR

Preheat oven to 350°. Lightly oil a 9 x 13 baking pan. In a large mixing bowl sift flour, sugar, baking soda and salt. Add fruit cocktail, with juice, and raisins. In a small bowl lightly beat eggs and add vanilla. Combine with flour mixture. Pour into baking pan and bake for 45 minutes or until done. Before slicing, sprinkle with powdered sugar.

Serves 10.

Arroz Dulce
(Rice Pudding)

1/2 cup MILK
1/2 cup RAISINS
3 cups cooked long-grain WHITE RICE
1 can (14 oz.) SWEETENED CONDENSED MILK
1/2 tsp. VANILLA
1/2 tsp. CINNAMON
1/4 tsp. NUTMEG

Combine all ingredients in a saucepan and stir over medium heat until mixture is thick. Serve warm or chill in refrigerator for 1 hour. To serve, place in individual serving bowls and sprinkle with nutmeg.

Serves 6.

Mexican Fruitcake

Cake:
- 2 cups FLOUR
- 2 cups SUGAR
- 2 EGGS
- 2 tsp. BAKING SODA
- 1/2 tsp. ALMOND EXTRACT
- 1/2 cup dried CHERRIES
- 1 can (20 oz.) crushed PINEAPPLE
- 1 cup chopped ALMONDS

Frosting:
- 1 pkg. (8 oz.) CREAM CHEESE, softened
- 2 cups POWDERED SUGAR
- 4 Tbsp. MARGARINE
- 1 tsp. ALMOND EXTRACT

Preheat oven to 350°. Blend cake ingredients together. Pour into a lightly greased 9 x 13 baking pan. Bake for 45 minutes. While cake is baking, prepare frosting by blending all ingredients together until smooth. Spread frosting on cake as soon as it comes out of the oven.

Serves 8.

Beverages

Traditional Margarita

4 oz. TEQUILA
2 oz. TRIPLE SEC®
2 cups LEMON-LIME MIX
COARSE SALT
ICE, crushed
LEMON or LIME wedges

Combine tequila, Triple Sec and lemon-lime mix in a cocktail shaker. Add ice and shake well. Rub lemon or lime wedge around glass rim and dip glass into salt (if desired). Strain the margaritas into two glasses.

Serves 2.

Margarita Punch

1 can (6 oz.) frozen LIMEADE concentrate
1 can (6 oz.) frozen LEMONADE concentrate
4 cups crushed ICE
1/2 cup POWDERED SUGAR
1 bottle (2-liter) GINGER ALE or CLUB SODA, chilled
2 cups TEQUILA
LIME wedges
COARSE SALT

In a blender combine limeade, lemonade, ice and powdered sugar. Blend until slushy. Pour into punch bowl and stir in ginger ale and tequila. When ready to serve, rub glass rims with lime wedges and dip glasses in salt (if desired).

Serves 16.

Rompope
(Rum Eggnog)

4 EGGS
1 can (14 oz.) SWEETENED CONDENSED MILK
1 tsp. VANILLA
1/2 tsp. CINNAMON
1/2 cup RUM
GROUND NUTMEG

Blend all ingredients (except for nutmeg) in a blender on high speed. Serve in small glasses with a sprinkle of nutmeg on top.

Serves 6.

Mexican Grasshopper

This is a great after-dinner drink

2 oz. KAHLUA
2 oz. CREME DE MENTHE
4 Tbsp. WHIPPING CREAM
ICE CUBES

Combine Kahlua, creme de menthe and whipping cream in a cocktail shaker with ice cubes. Shake well and strain into cocktail glasses.

Serves 2.

Kahlua Colada

1 oz. KAHLUA
1/2 oz. RUM
1 oz. CREAM OF COCONUT
2 oz. PINEAPPLE JUICE
1 cup CRUSHED ICE

Blend all ingredients and serve in a tall chilled glass.

Serves 1.

Sangrita

3 cups V-8® JUICE
1/2 cup ORANGE JUICE
2 Tbsp. LIME JUICE
2 oz. diced GREEN CHILES

1 Tbsp. SUGAR
1 tsp. WORCESTERSHIRE SAUCE
TABASCO® to taste
1/4 tsp. ONION POWDER

Combine all ingredients in blender and blend until smooth. Chill and serve in tall glasses over ice. Garnish with **CELERY STALK** in each glass.

Serves 6.

Sangría

A red wine punch of Spanish origin.

1 cup SUGAR
4 cups WATER
4 cups ORANGE JUICE
4 cups RED WINE

1 cup BRANDY
1 ORANGE, sliced
crushed ICE

In a large punch bowl dissolve sugar in water. Add juice, wine and brandy. Cover and chill. Before serving, float orange slices on top. Pour over crushed ice in tall glasses.

Serves 12.

Tequila Sunrise

2 oz. TEQUILA
1/2 cup ORANGE JUICE
1 Tbsp. GRENADINE

1 Tsp. LIME JUICE
ICE, crushed
MARASCHINO CHERRY

Combine tequila, orange juice, grenadine and lime juice in blender and blend. Pour into tall glass over crushed ice. Garnish with cherry.

Serves 1.

Refresco de Fresas

(Strawberry Drink)

1 basket STRAWBERRIES
6 cups WATER
1/2 cup SUGAR
crushed ICE

Hull and slice strawberries, add with 2 cups water to blender and purée. Add remaining water and sugar and mix thoroughly. Cover and refrigerate. To serve, pour over crushed ice in tall glasses. If desired, garnish with **MINT sprigs.**

Mexican Hot Chocolate

1/2 cup COCOA POWDER
1/2 cup MASA HARINA
6 cups MILK

1 tsp. VANILLA
1 cup SUGAR
6 CINNAMON STICKS

In a large saucepan, combine cocoa, masa harina, milk, vanilla and sugar and blend well. Simmer over medium heat, stirring constantly until thickened. Pour into mugs and serve with cinnamon sticks.

Serves 6.

Mexican Mocha

4 cups COFFEE (instant or brewed)
2 cups MILK
1/2 cup COCOA POWDER

2 Tbsp. SUGAR
1/2 tsp. VANILLA
1/4 tsp. CINNAMON

In a large saucepan, combine coffee, milk, cocoa powder and sugar and bring to a boil. Remove from heat and add vanilla and cinnamon. Pour into a blender and process on high until frothy. Serve hot.

Serves 6.

Cafe de Almendra
(Almond Coffee)

1 cup hot COFFEE
1 oz. AMARETTO
4 oz. VANILLA ICE CREAM
CINNAMON

In a large coffee mug, combine coffee and amaretto. Spoon in ice cream and sprinkle with cinnamon.

Serves 1.

Cafe Mexicano
(Mexican Coffee)

1 cup hot COFFEE
1 oz. KAHLUA
1/2 oz. TEQUILA
1 tsp. BROWN SUGAR
CINNAMON

Combine all ingredients in a large coffee mug.

Serves 1.

Chile Glossary

Anaheim: Also called "California" or "California green chiles". These are mild long chiles which are closely related to the *New Mexico chile.* These chiles are great for stuffing *(rellenos)* and can be used to make a mild green sauce with tomatillos. The red, dried form is most often seen hanging in "ristras." The red is sweeter than the green.

Ancho: A dried *poblano* chile. The most commonly used dried chile in Mexico. It is a very dark red (almost black) when dried. Used in tamales, menudo and many sauces.

Cayenne: Used most often in powdered form as a seasoning. Usually 2-4 inches long, bright red and tapering to a point. Very hot.

Chiltepin: A wild form of the *pequín.* Medium red, oval-shaped and about the size of a marble. This dried chile is very hot.

Chipotle: A dried, smoked jalapeño. The flavor is smoky, pungent and very hot.

Habanero: The hottest chile in the world! This lantern-shaped, 2-inch long chile ranges from dark green to orange-red to red in color. It is used in salsas, chutneys and marinades and is sometimes pickled.

Jalapeño: Bright medium to dark green, about 2-3 inches long, tapering to a rounded end. The most popular hot chile in the United States. Can be eaten raw, pickled, roasted and is available canned.

New Mexico: Slightly hotter than the *Anaheim chile,* utilized the same way. The dried red chiles can be seen hanging in "ristras" throughout the Southwest.

Pasilla: Also called *chile negro,* it is a dried *chilaca chile.* Dark brown, wrinkled, tapered, and about 5-6 inches long. Used in making sauces.

Poblano: One of the most popular fresh chiles in Mexico. These chiles are triangular in shape, dark green, about 4-5 inches long and 2-3 inches in diameter. Used cooked or roasted. Excellent for *chiles rellenos.*

Serrano: The hottest chile commonly available in the U.S. This smooth-skinned green and red chile is used in sauces and salsas.

Tabasco: Bright orange-red, about 1 1/2 inches long. Very hot. Used primarily in Tabasco® sauces.

Index

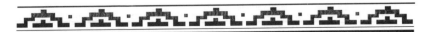

About the Authors

Shayne and Lee Fischer are natives of Arizona. Both grew up with an affinity for Mexican foods. Lee remembers the first restaurant he ever went to was a Mexican food restaurant. Shayne's early love for Mexican food was sparked by her mother's homemade tacos. As both Shayne and Lee are lacto-ovo vegetarians, they adapted traditional Mexican recipes to reflect their meat-free lifestyle.

Although not all of the recipes in this book are authentic Mexican recipes, they represent the Mexican style of cooking and fit into today's health-conscious lifestyles. As health and exercise enthusiasts, Shayne and Lee found it necessary to create these recipes so they could indulge more often in their favorite pastime, eating Mexican food!

Authors of five other cookbooks: *Berry Lovers Cook Book, Burrito Lovers Cook Book, Low Fat Mexican Recipes, Wholly Frijoles* (by Shayne) and *Bean Lovers Cook Book* (by Shayne), the Fischers live in Phoenix where they continue to pursue an active lifestyle which includes power walking, running, bicycling, hiking and eating Mexican food.

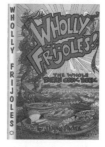

ORDER BLANK

GOLDEN WEST PUBLISHERS

☼ 4113 N. Longview Ave. • Phoenix, AZ 85014

www.goldenwestpublishers.com • **1-800-658-5830** • FAX 602-279-6901

Qty	Title	Price	Amount
	Bean Lovers Cook Book	6.95	
	Berry Lovers Cook Book	6.95	
	Best Barbecue Recipes	6.95	
	Burrito Lovers Cook Book	6.95	
	Chili-Lovers' Cook Book	6.95	
	Chip and Dip Lovers Cook Book	6.95	
	Cowboy Cartoon Cook Book	7.95	
	Gourmet Gringo Cook Book	14.95	
	Grand Canyon Cook Book	6.95	
	Low Fat Mexican Recipes	6.95	
	Mexican Desserts & Drinks	6.95	
	Quick-n-Easy Mexican Recipes	6.95	
	Real New Mexico Chile	6.95	
	Recipes for a Healthy Lifestyle	6.95	
	Salsa Lovers Cook Book	6.95	
	Tequila Cook Book	7.95	
	Tortilla Lovers Cook Book	6.95	
	Veggie Lovers Cook Book	6.95	
	Vegi-Mex: Vegetarian Mexican Recipes	6.95	
	Wholly Frijoles! The Whole Bean Book	6.95	
Shipping & Handling Add:	United States $3.00 Canada & Mexico $5.00—All others $12.00		

☐ My Check or Money Order Enclosed

☐ MasterCard ☐ VISA ($20 credit card minimum)

Total $ _____

(Payable in U.S. funds)

Acct. No. _____ Exp. Date _____

Signature _____

Name _____ Phone _____

Address _____

City/State/Zip _____

Call for a FREE catalog of all of our titles

8/02   **This order blank may be photocopied**   Vegi-Mex